DIGITAL HUMANITIES

This book offers an accessible introduction to the digital humanities, with a particular focus on literary studies. It explains key debates and definitions of digital humanities, tracing the field from its origins in Father Roberto Busa's pioneering computational work on the texts of Thomas Aquinas in the 1940s through to the challenges and possibilities posed by artificial intelligence and generative technologies today.

Beginning with the question of what work in the digital humanities entails, James O'Sullivan moves through the field's defining tensions. He introduces computational approaches to text analysis and distant reading before turning to digital literature, examining the arc from early hypertext fiction to contemporary interactive and generative works. The discussion extends into publishing in the digital age, including social media, open access, and digital editions. Throughout, the book confronts the field's shortcomings, including persistent inequalities of race, gender, and labour. Written for students, researchers, and anyone curious about how computing is reshaping the study of culture, this concise guide will be of particular value to those in literary studies, cultural criticism, and the broader humanities who wish to engage critically with digital tools and methods.

James O'Sullivan is Professor of Digital Culture & Cultural Analytics at University College Cork, Ireland, where he conducts empirical research on literature and explores the changing nature of culture and cultural production in the digital age.

THE NEW CRITICAL IDIOM

SERIES EDITOR: JOHN DRAKAKIS, UNIVERSITY OF STIRLING

The New Critical Idiom is an invaluable series of introductory guides to today's critical terminology. Each book:

- provides a handy, explanatory guide to the use (and abuse) of the term;
- offers an original and distinctive overview by a leading literary and cultural critic;
- relates the term to the larger field of cultural representation.

With a strong emphasis on clarity, lively debate and the widest possible breadth of examples, *The New Critical Idiom* is an indispensable approach to key topics in literary studies.

Fictionality
Karen Petroski

Tragedy
John Drakakis

Travel Writing
Second Edition
Carl Thompson

The Historical Novel
Second Edition
Jerome de Groot

Grotesque
Second Edition
Justin D. Edwards and Rune Graulund

Digital Humanities
James O'Sullivan

For more information about this series, please visit: www.routledge.com/The-New-Critical-Idiom/book-series/SE0155

DIGITAL HUMANITIES

James O'Sullivan

Routledge
Taylor & Francis Group
LONDON AND NEW YORK

Designed cover image: Getty Images

First published 2027
by Routledge
4 Park Square, Milton Park, Abingdon, Oxon OX14 4RN

and by Routledge
605 Third Avenue, New York, NY 10158

Routledge is an imprint of the Taylor & Francis Group, an informa business

British Library Cataloguing-in-Publication Data
A catalogue record for this book is available from the British Library

Library of Congress Cataloging-in-Publication Data
Names: O'Sullivan, James Christopher author
Title: Digital humanities / James O'Sullivan.
Description: Abingdon, Oxon ; New York, NY : Routledge, 2027. |
Series: The new critical idiom | Includes bibliographical references and index. |
Identifiers: LCCN 2026019145 (print) | LCCN 2026019146 (ebook) |
ISBN 9780815384793 hbk | ISBN 9780815384809 pbk | ISBN 9781351203395 ebk
Subjects: LCSH: Digital humanities
Classification: LCC AZ105 .O78 2027 (print) | LCC AZ105 (ebook) |
DDC 001.30285--dc23/eng/20260603
LC record available at https://lccn.loc.gov/2026019145
LC ebook record available at https://lccn.loc.gov/2026019146

ISBN: 978-0-815-38479-3 (hbk)
ISBN: 978-0-815-38480-9 (pbk)
ISBN: 978-1-351-20339-5 (ebk)

DOI: 10.4324/9781351203395

Typeset in Times New Roman
by Taylor & Francis Books

For my father, John—
whom I miss every day.

Contents

Series Editor's Preface

The New Critical Idiom is a series of introductory books which seeks to extend the lexicon of literary terms, in order to address the radical changes which have taken place in the study of literature during the last decades of the twentieth century. The aim is to provide clear, well-illustrated accounts of the full range of terminology currently in use, and to evolve histories of its changing usage.

The current state of the discipline of literary studies is one where there is considerable debate concerning basic questions of terminology. This involves, among other things: the boundaries which distinguish the literary from the non-literary; the position of literature within the larger sphere of culture; the relationship between literatures of different cultures; and questions concerning the relation of literary to other cultural forms within the context of interdisciplinary studies.

It is clear that the field of literary criticism and theory is a dynamic and heterogeneous one. The present need is for individual volumes on terms which combine clarity of exposition with an adventurousness of perspective and a breadth of application. Each volume will contain as part of its apparatus some indication of the direction in which the definition of particular terms is likely to move, as well as expanding the disciplinary boundaries within which some of these terms have been traditionally contained. This will involve some re-situation of terms within the larger field of cultural representation, and will introduce examples from the area of film and the modern media in addition to examples from a variety of literary texts.

1

WHAT ARE THE DIGITAL HUMANITIES?

There is a piazza in Rome which, unless purposely sought, seems much like the many others scattered throughout the Italian capital. It is, in a city that boasts such attractions as Piazza Navona, Piazza San Pietro, Piazza del Popolo and Piazza di Spagna, all steeped in elegance, history and charm, something of a nonentity. This little-known cobbled square, Piazza della Pilotta, has no fountains or obelisks to offer its pedestrians, featuring instead the faded blue markings of a car park, set out before two unremarkable buildings which act as boundaries to the north and south. Its western wall is more interesting, for here stands the Pontifical Biblical Institute, identified by its distinctively orange façade. The striking Institute may well give anyone who has chanced upon this place some pause, but it is the building on the opposite eastern edge of the square which holds significance for readers of this book—the Gregoriana, the site where, according to many, the digital humanities were born.

This story has been told a thousand times, most thoroughly by Steven E. Jones who begins not in Rome but on the streets of New York during one of its signature ticker-tape parades

DOI: 10.4324/9781351203395-1

(Jones 2016, 27). Jones begins his disciplinary history with a joke, of the timeless "a man walks into a bar" sort, but on this occasion the man is a priest, and the bar is a CEO's office, 59 Madison Avenue, the then and now international headquarters of IBM. The year is 1949, and Thomas J. Watson Sr., to whom the office belongs, is in the twilight of his stewardship of the company he founded alongside Charles Ranlett Flint in 1911. The priest is Father Roberto Busa, an Italian Jesuit who had recently finished a thesis, *The Thomistic Terminology of Interiority*, at the aforementioned Papal Gregorian University, work which examined *specific* Latin words in context through the use of handwritten index cards (Jones 2016, 28).

Busa was eying a far grander project when he walked into Watson's office, a complete index, or index verborum, of *all* the words—every single one—contained within the works of Saint Thomas Aquinas, a corpus of some eleven million words of medieval Latin (Hockey 2004, 4). Decades later, Busa's vision would be realised as the *Index Thomisticus*,[1] a lemmatised concordance of Aquinas' *oeuvre* which, using punched cards, allowed users to see where particular words or word forms occur within the corpus. Busa did not invent the concordance, but he did lead one of the first major data processing projects to treat cultural materials; he had the vision to use punched cards—how digital data was represented and stored at the time—to effectively turn the works of Aquinas into machine-readable text that could be analysed using automated and semi-automated procedures. The *Index Thomisticus* was one of the first projects to apply computer technologies in "dealing with unstructured language" (Rockwell and Passarotti 2019, 15), and as such, many now consider it among the first endeavours in what are now known as the "digital humanities," or more colloquially, "DH."

There are many genealogies of DH, the specifics of which will often differ depending on the national and cultural contexts involved. Any one practitioner's take on what constitutes a legitimate digital humanities origin story will be informed by their own interests and institutional frames. But it is difficult to dispute that the Busa narrative is *the* popular genealogy; it is almost a folktale, and folktales are useful in that they tell us something essential of the communities from which they have emerged. And what the Busa story tells us about DH is at once useful and problematic—*DH is not for everyone.*

The prevailing discourse around DH is that anyone can do it; one must simply find a suitably intuitive tool for visualisation making or install a platform and build a website. But this perspective greatly diminishes the legitimacy of the digital humanities by allowing its intellectual foundations to be diluted by those who see value in aligning with the discipline merely because it is fashionable to do so. Or certainly, it was useful to do so; increasingly, "DH" is becoming replaced with terms like "cultural analytics," or scholars that once identified as DH are now turning to "artificial intelligence" ("critical AI," anyone?). The term "computational humanities" has emerged in recent times, signalling a desire by some cohorts to return to the beginnings of DH, to the "humanities computing" (before all new media and cultural studies found their way into the tent).

In some respects, this book is arriving late in the day; the digital humanities are, after all, semi-normal, if not, at this stage, entirely normal (Underwood 2019; Drucker 2023). But in other ways, now is the perfect time for this book's arrival, because the aforementioned terminological fragmentation reflects a deeper tension within the digital humanities: the struggle to balance intellectual cohesion with the field's celebrated plurality. The emergence of terms like "cultural analytics" and "computational humanities" signifies a maturing discipline, one that recognises and has finally accepted its diversity and seeks to articulate distinct strands within its practice. But these shifts risk exacerbating the sense of fragmentation, as different cohorts stake claims to what DH is—or should be—without fully addressing its broader intellectual mission (which has been a common problem in this field for the best part of two decades).

While early humanities computing focused on text analysis and encoding, the digital humanities have since grown into an interdisciplinary space that embraces questions of power, identity, and representation in the digital age. Susan Schreibman, Ray Siemens and John Unsworth are largely recognised for having legitimised the term "digital humanities" around the turn of the century.

Tasked with the process of editing what would become Blackwell's seminal *A Companion to Digital Humanities*, Schreibman, Siemens and Unsworth wanted a more expansive term for their discipline, one which "broadened its reach" while still retaining "the goals that animated it from the outset." Those goals were listed as the use of "information technology to illuminate the human record, and bringing an understanding of the human record to bear on the development and use of information technology" (Schreibman 2004). Dave Parry argues that the rhetorical shift from "humanities computing" to "digital humanities" is useful in that it seems less threatening to traditional scholarship (Parry 2012). There are scholars who see "humanities computing" as a more accurate representation of the computer-heavy activities with which they are engaged; "digital humanities" being better suited to the "newer" form of DH, rife with theory and cultural studies. But whatever one calls it, institutionally speaking, the term "digital humanities," at least for the best part of the last two decades, seems to have stuck (though as noted, this may now be shifting once more).

Retreating to an earlier, ostensibly more technical characterisations of the field risks undoing the progress made in integrating the humanities' critical sensibilities into computational work, but equally, a truly representative DH is one in which equal space has been made for the technical (because as will be seen, that kind of DH is *extremely* valuable). Simultaneously, the pivot toward artificial intelligence reflects a pragmatic response to the shifting priorities of academic institutions and funding bodies, much like everyone was once pivoting to DH. And while it is fair to say that generative AI and machine learning offer new opportunities for DH to push methodological boundaries, they also bring challenges. Just as it once was with DH, scholars are facing increasing pressure to position their work within the discourse of AI, often at the expense of the humanistic inquiry that should remain central. Terms like critical AI attempt to bridge this divide, but they risk becoming buzzwords—just as DH was once a buzzword—more reflective of institutional branding than substantive engagement and disciplinary excellence.

Of course, the digital humanities, and other disciplines within the humanities and social sciences, have been before, and what unites these divergent trends is the persistent question of DH's identity. And that, essentially, is what this book is about. In the present age—the age of ubiquitous screens, data science, and intelligent machines—what does it mean to do digital humanities? What does it mean to do work in the humanities, to think and communicate critically, in a way that is mediated, very explicitly, through computers? Such work is not exclusive to the digital humanities, but all forms of digital humanities, do this kind of work. And so, while it would be a disservice to each field to suggest that "computational humanities," "cultural analytics," and "critical AI" can be used interchangeably, there are commonalities between each of these domains and the digital humanities, and oftentimes, the people and practices that make up one will be indistinguishable from the other. Some of these commonalities are what this book introduces, the interplay between the humanities and computing, and what it means to operate as a theorist and critic and the juncture between these two disciplinary cultures.

THE DH NEXUS

Roberto Busa was positioned to become one of the first scholars of the digital humanities because he enjoyed considerable privilege, but also because he had a genuine appreciation of how the technologies of the day could be used to fundamentally advance his text-based research. His story is the ideal parable for all that is right and wrong with DH.

Roberto Busa was a visionary. We know this because he himself did not possess the specific expertise necessary to fulfil his ambition. Jones details how unlikely it is that Busa "knew the full scope and difficulty of the task he was facing," but that he nonetheless understood the "essential components" of what he needed to automate the processing of his textual data (Jones 2016, 30). We see Busa's lack of technical expertise reflected in his vague technical vocabulary, his reference to "some type of machinery" (Busa 1980, 83) and "gadgets" (Jones 2016, 28).

Seeing beyond the technicalities of what one cannot fully understand is the hallmark of the visionary, and without knowing precisely how the machines he needed would work, Busa knew it was machines that he needed. The DH origin story is full of such visionaries, people who anticipated the emergence of computer-assisted criticism long before its time, even long before computer scientists. The Women Writers Project was founded in 1986 at Brown University with the intention of making available in electronic form the texts of forgotten early modern women writers. The project's first director, Susanne Woods, foresaw "that the computer could do interesting things with texts," but like Busa, she "was not sure what" (Woods 1994, 18).

Busa bears a further, somewhat murkier hallmark of the visionary: his ideas enjoyed the privilege necessary to see them cultivated. Figures like Busa and Woods have given great service to DH by showing acolytes and detractors alike what can be achieved through the application of computers to humanities research, but they also share a commonality in that their pioneering was accomplished at a time when they enjoyed affiliations with some of the world's most powerful and affluent organisations. How many visionaries have been forgotten because they did not have the resources of Brown University or IBM? How many potential origins have remained unrealised because they had no Thomas Watson? It is doubtful that Busa would have been able to gather the referrals necessary to set a meeting with one of the world's most powerful businessmen had he not been a Jesuit (Jones 2016, 31), and as for Watson, when the pair met the IBM CEO had just led his company through some highly profitable dealings with Nazi Germany (Black 2001). One of the first great projects of the digital humanities required collaboration between the Church and IBM, showing how the field's problematic interactions with various social, intellectual, and economic dynamics were present from its very beginnings.[2]

In demonstrating the vast resources needed to complete a project of the scope of the *Index Thomisticus*, the Busa-centric origin story shows how DH can be an exclusionary space. Whatever the corroborative or alternative histories of DH, and there are many,[3] the dominance of this particular folktale, made possible by two organisations whose resources and influence were inimically achieved, shows how the present moment is one in which certain types of projects can only be accomplished by those with access to suitable resources. And yet, despite these limitations, and despite most practitioners of DH not enjoying the support of clergies, CEOs, and Ivy League schools, the digital humanities are flourishing. And it is because they flourish, because the landscape has changed so much since Busa, and indeed, continues to change with each new generation of DH (or cultural analytics, or computational humanities, or critical AI) practitioner, that we must retrace old ground, return to that tired but important question: what exactly is this thing called DH?

In 2012, Kathleen Fitzpatrick asked whether "digital humanities" should be singular or plural. Referring to preparations for a lunchtime talk, Fitzpatrick notes how the precis of a lecture she was developing evolved from "what is digital humanities?" to "what is *the* digital humanities?" to "what *are* the digital humanities?" (Fitzpatrick 2012). Having first registered her indecision as an unremarkable moment of grammatical uncertainty, Fitzpatrick later recognised the conceptual muddle that had led to her ambivalence: when we refer to "digital humanities," do we mean one discipline, or a set of disciplines? Fitzpatrick had already made a first attempt at answering that question two years before, when she wrote that DH is:

> a nexus of fields within which scholars use computing technologies to investigate the kinds of questions that are traditional to the humanities, or, as is more true of my own work, ask traditional kinds of humanities-oriented questions about computing technologies.
>
> (Fitzpatrick 2010)

And here we are, over a decade since Fitzpatrick penned her eloquent definition, and we are still asking "what is DH?"

The operative term in Fitzpatrick's definition is "fields," her use of the plural showing how she was already convinced of DH as a *set* of disciplines before she had explicitly queried her thinking. In the present moment, it is unthinkable that we would consider the digital humanities as anything but plural. While DH first emerged out of text analysis, we are now seeing scholars from all corners of the humanities identify with this intellectual turn. Fitzpatrick observes:

> Digital humanities as it is currently practiced isn't just located in literary studies departments; the field is broadly humanities based and includes scholars in history, musicology, performance studies, media studies, and other fields that can benefit from bringing computing technologies to bear on traditional humanities materials.
>
> (Fitzpatrick 2010)

Text analysis—which incorporates fields like computational literary studies—still dominates major international gatherings of DH scholars but the nexus, as Fitzpatrick calls it, has grown considerably. The digital humanities have progressed from the priest and his punched cards to a riot of differing materials, perspectives and practices.

That DH is now recognised as something of a "big tent"[4] is both a strength and weakness; it allows practitioners to embrace plurality, but it also encourages a type of "tactical convenience." The idea of DH as "tactical" has been most notably developed by Matthew Kirschenbaum across a trilogy of famous essays (Kirschenbaum 2012a; 2012b; 2014). In the most iconic of the three, "What Is Digital Humanities and What's It Doing in English Departments?," Kirschenbaum describes the emergence of a new generation of scholars determined to use "digital humanities" partly as a label designed to improve their prospects in the increasingly precarious academic job market:[5]

> Digital humanities has also, I would propose, lately been galvanized by a group of younger (or not so young) graduate students, faculty members (both tenure line and contingent), and other academic professionals who now wield the label "digital humanities" instrumentally amid an increasingly monstrous institutional terrain defined by declining public support for higher education, rising tuitions, shrinking endowments, the proliferation of distance education and the for-profit university, and underlying it all the conversion of full-time, tenure-track academic labor to a part-time adjunct workforce.
>
> (Kirschenbaum 2012b)

The instrumentality of DH—of using computers in the humanities—has been reinforced in recent years as our institutions have become even more monstrous. Back in 2012, the term DH was "unabashedly deployed" (2012a), and while it now has some bedfellows (again, cultural analytics, computational humanities, critical AI), the trend has not abated. If one is to "get things done," one needs a measure of DH (2012a). Such tactical convenience is not exclusive to DH, and the history of academic disciplines is littered with "dependencies between its intellectual currency and bottom-line ways and means" (Kirschenbaum 2014, 55). It is easy to envisage a future in which digital forms of humanities pass the baton to environmental or medical humanities, but right now, if one is to be tactical, they need to be doing things with computers.

It is easy to sympathise with a desperation for alignment: people need opportunities if they are to begin and develop careers, they need strategies if they are to survive precarity. And historically it has sometimes been those in the most precarious positions who have advanced disciplines. Digital humanities, it might be argued, emerged out of a need for something different, and continues to grow because that demand remains unsatisfied. But balance is needed: the digital humanities will flourish if allowed to remain plural (Fitzpatrick 2012), but DH must resist becoming a fashionable catch-all that only serves professional convenience. If this discipline is to be something then it needs lines of demarcation: students and publics do not really care about the politics of disciplinary alignment, they want to know what DH is all about, why they or others might perceive it as a valuable endeavour (and we will get to that). Such boundaries have been and are problematic and will need to be repeatedly redrawn in the years to come, but they must exist, not so any sense of plurality might be suffocated, but so that the idea of a plural DH might be meaningful.

NOT EVERYONE USING A COMPUTER IS DOING DH

It has been over two decades since John Unsworth suggested that the digital humanities were suffering from an influx of what he calls—citing Tito Orlandi, yet another Italian pioneer of DH

(Nyhan and Flinn 2016b)—"charlatans." The Unsworthian charlatan personifies an overly plural DH, conflating all computer-based activities as being critically equal:

> All our activities may all look the same, and they may all take place in the same interface, the same ›discourse universe‹ of icons, menus, and behaviors, but they're not all equally valuable, they don't all work on the same assumptions – they're not, in fact, interchangeable. To put a more narrowly academic focus on all this, I would hazard a guess that everyone reading this uses a word-processor and email as basic tools of the profession, and I expect that many readers are also in the humanities. Even so, you do not all do humanities computing – nor should you, for heaven's sake – any more than you should all be medievalists, or modernists, or linguists.
>
> (Unsworth 2002)

Just because you are using a computer does not mean you are doing digital humanities, just as using ChatGPT does not make you an expert in artificial intelligence. We want a plural DH, but if everyone using a computer is a digital humanities scholar then the digital humanities are everything and thus nothing.

It may seem wearisome to revive the "not everyone using a computer is doing DH" mantra, but it has never been more pertinent. The international humanities are now over a decade into what Matthew Gold describes as "the DH moment" (Gold 2012b), and have witnessed, and continue to witness, an increasing number of programmes, positions and projects which describe themselves as being digital humanities.

Nowhere is this more prevalent than in the rise of "the DH job," typically "alt-ac" positions designed to support the development of digital scholarship within a specific institutional context (O'Sullivan 2018b). Those who find themselves in such employment spend a great deal of time fielding questions on how to use social media and build websites, queries which would be more appropriately directed to the nearest teenager. Unless the intellectual practices of the digital humanities are routinely made explicit, the field will stand for little more than a catch-all for web-based marketing activities. Charlatanism has made headway because of a culture of ignorance, a culture in which institutions and colleagues confuse DH with the use of general web tools and services that have absolutely nothing at all to do with *scholarship.* Of course, the confused colleague is not the worst offender, the real charlatan is the scholar who relies on the labour of others or black-box tools to pose as an expert in DH, hiding a dearth of appreciation for the methodological underpinnings or intellectual consequences of such practices. The true charlatans are those DH scholars whose work could really be done without any mention of the digital, work which they only call DH because, returning full circle to Kirschenbaum, it is convenient for them to do so.

This is not a call for a witch hunt; approaching the "what is DH?" conversation from the perspective of the field's archetypal practitioners is a useful way of explaining its emergence and current state. If someone wants to see what the digital humanities are all about, they should look to those who are doing relevant work. One might count five types of people doing DH: the charlatan, the pioneer, the DH-curious, the converted, and the specialist.

The charlatan, already discussed, is the scholar who sees DH as a means to some other end. The hope is that, as the field continues to mature and we all gain a greater sense of what we expect intellectually rigorous DH to entail, their numbers will dwindle. It is quite possible that we have already reached this point, that the days of "Tweesays" counting as scholarship are now at their end.

The pioneers are those scholars who define a generation, iterating the field through radical contributions, showing us new ways in which computers can contribute to our exploration of the arts and humanities. If one traces the development of any intellectual field, they will see the pioneers, the thinkers and practitioners who reoriented the occupations and practices of a discipline. Pioneers define their generation, establishing the broad epistemic trends which their peers will follow until other pioneers and generations emerge to take their place. Broadly speaking, the digital humanities have had two generations: the early pioneers of humanities computing who were largely occupied with statistical analysis and adapting the emerging web to activities like text encoding, and the more recent, broader church of DH which incorporates scholars with an interest in computers beyond what they can provide as analytical tools. Of course, generations can co-exist; computers and mainframes were not shut down simply because a new wave of DH scholars with interests in social and cultural theory emerged. And many (if not most) pioneers are never recognised.

Generally, though, looking to the pioneers of DH yields some sense of how the field has developed. The first generation of DH, at least, as it existed in the Anglophone world, was typified by figures like Geoffrey Rockwell and Stéfan Sinclair, the creators of Voyant Tools, a hugely popular text analytics platform; John Burrows, whose work remains central to computer-assisted analyses of literary style; and Julia Flanders, who has been a major contributor to the Women Writers Project and Text Encoding Initiative since the early nineties. That first generation was very much about text.

It might be expected that the emergence of the second generation coincided with the shift in terminology from "humanities computing" to "digital humanities" around the turn of the century. However, it was not until later, around 2012 or so, that a pronounced body of DH scholarship aligned with social and cultural studies, even activism, came to the fore. This move towards DH-beyond-statistics was pioneered by figures like Lisa Spiro, whose famed "This Is Why We Fight" essay on the ethics and values of DH was hailed as something of a turning point (2012); Alan Liu, who accused the digital humanities of being oblivious to cultural criticism (2012); and Roopika Risam, whose major work centres on postcolonial digital humanities (2018). In fact, much of the second generation seems rooted in the *Debates in the Digital Humanities* series and its publications which have privileged DH as cultural criticism (Gold 2012a; Gold and Klein 2016; 2019), and more recently, intersectional and feminist DH (Losh and Wernimont 2019), and Black Atlantic studies (Risam and Josephs 2021). DH-as-text-analysis, or what is now often referred to as cultural analytics or computational humanities/computational literary studies, has also enjoyed some new pioneers: scholars like Maciej Eder, Karina van Dalen-Oskam, Christof Schöch, Barbara McGillivray, Ted Underwood, and Andrew Piper have transformed quantitative approaches to text (largely literary) analysis.

The first generation of humanities computing really had two second generations: those carrying on the discipline's foundational work, the application of computers to the analysis of culture, and those looking to use DH for the purposes of cultural criticism and social justice. And it might be argued, that somewhere between the two groups, sit pioneering librarians and a third second generation of pioneers.

But whatever the specific focus of their work, it is the pioneers who have made DH what it is, and indeed, in time they will remake it once more. In all honesty, to answer the question, "what are the digital humanities?," one need only put down this book and use those names mentioned in the preceding paragraphs to guide their reading—theirs is the work of the digital humanities.

Pioneers are rare. Far more common are the DH-curious, those without advanced expertise but a healthy desire to know more about the discipline and whether it is of relevance to their research interests. The DH-curious are different from the charlatans in that they are honest about their motives and abilities, and do not presume to know what "real" DH might look like, though they are eager to form an impression. One does not belong to this category for long, either retreating from the field or graduating to the converted.

Some of the greatest contributors to DH come from the converted category, the group of scholars who rarely possess formal training in a technical discipline, but who started out in the arts and humanities and picked up the digital part of their practice at some later stage. The converted differ from the DH-curious in that they have persisted with their own individual development, the hallmark of this group being their deep appreciation of how technical disciplines can interact with the arts and humanities. Many pioneers come from the converted. In most disciplines, the most common—and arguably most important—persona is that of the worker, professional scholars and practitioners who do not redefine their fields, but rather, attend the vital business of everyday research and teaching. The DH converted are the field's workers, those who sustain the digital humanities and make them tick.

The specialists are a direct consequence of the DH moment, students and scholars who have been educated in DH-heavy or DH-specific programmes and see themselves less as interdisciplinary, and more as "just DH." They do not see DH as a toolkit to be applied to cognate disciplines within the arts and humanities, but rather as an intrinsic part of humanistic rationale. The figure of the converted versus that of the specialist is really a reflection on the nature of interdisciplinarity as it exists in higher education: DH *must* be interdisciplinary, but how that happens, how a scholar goes from using machine learning to study cultural materials and whether that is something they always did or will come to later, indicates the difference between the converted and the specialists. We can consider the specialists to be those scholars who have never really known or had a concern for a subject from the arts and humanities without the involvement of the digital; their reading has always been computer-assisted.

Considering which of these archetypes will dominate the coming decade is a useful way of considering the future of the digital humanities. It is a common suggestion that sophisticated computational techniques will just fold seamlessly into the lifecycle of all humanities scholars at some point, effacing the current distinction between the digital and wider humanities. This position seems to ignore the exponential rate at which computers evolve, and there is still so much to be achieved that one struggles to see a time when the digital humanities will not require its own, dedicated community of experts responsible for the further advancements of tools and techniques designed to ask complex questions of the great many rich and multifaceted artefacts which humans and cultures produce. What is considered computationally "sophisticated" today will have changed tomorrow, and that change, as in any discipline, will be brought about by subject specialists. It will be intriguing to see whether the future belongs to the converted or to the specialists, whether DH will continue to be best served by scholars who turn a little curiosity into an additional specialism, or by those who have only ever known the humanities as digital and interdisciplinary.

Many digital humanities scholars might also fall neatly into Quinn Dombrowski's "technical enough" category (Dombrowski 2019), not possessing technical acumen equivalent to that of a software engineer, but nonetheless having the curiosity and persistence necessary to generate a knowledge that will have considerable professional utility and value. In fact, Dombrowski's more binary system of classification may well be all there is to it: good digital humanities scholars are those who are "technical enough." Those who are not technical enough, do not do DH. Many digital humanities scholars might feel that they are sharing in the fate of Karl Marx, who once quipped that economists think him a great philosopher, while philosophers think him a great economist.

But what does any of this matter when, in the twenty-first century, it is hardly surprising that a new generation of scholars has emerged with a desire to synthesise a love of fiction or history with a fondness for computers and screens? Furthermore, most students of DH, certainly the undergraduates, do not even care about the term "digital humanities" and what it might or might not entail (Cordell 2016). Much like the DH-curious scholars who care only about the instrumental value of the discipline, they have no appetite for meta-discussions of epistemology. Mark Sample once tweeted that the digital humanities are "something white tenured males have the privilege to debate on Twitter," expressing what is increasingly becoming a common sentiment: what is the point of defining DH, and does anyone really care about doing so? In 2017, Ian Bogost went viral with his own "It's 2017 and still nobody knows what Digital Humanities is" tweet, teasing those scholars who continue to ask what seems to some a hollow pursuit.

Sarah Stanley likens the "what is DH?" debate to "navel-gazing," and that continually returning to the matter serves little function if it does not actually inform the way DH is practised in real terms (Stanley 2017). Stanley argues that there would be far more utility in asking, "why is DH?," treating the intellectual and institutional conditions which gave rise to the DH moment. Approaching DH from such a perspective, one comes to appreciate the field through a descriptive examination of its disciplinary practices, rather than the typical, more prescriptive theoretical treatments to which Stanley is reacting. In answering the "Why DH?" question, Stanley presents the field as a response to outmoded institutional practices and hierarchies, as a response to changing modes of production, a lack of structural support for interdisciplinarity, unsustainable infrastructures, and the inequitable recognition of labour. Asking "why?" instead of "what?" leads to community definitions derived from assessments of what is being done by *everyone* who identifies as part of that community, which Stanley asserts is how we position ourselves to address "the needs and concerns of our community and engaging in a bottom-up approach to knowledge-making" (Stanley 2017).

Perhaps the disquiet around the rapid emergence of the digital humanities has died down, that the naysayers are accepting it, and that everyone is just getting on about their business—digital humanities is now normal, so we no longer need to ask "what" or "why" (Underwood 2019; Drucker 2023). Or perhaps the rise of generative AI has stolen its thunder, and DH can finally join the rest of the humanities on the margins of institutional priorities. Ted Underwood argues that we must resist a return to the old days, being drawn into a debate about who is or is not a digital humanist (Underwood 2017; 2019). While some measure of debate over identity and purpose is inevitable in any discipline—scholars in literary studies have long been occupied with self-definition (Cain 2001; Hewson 2018) while an essay by the historian Kenneth May, written in the mid-seventies, could not have more resonance today: "What is good history and who should do it?" (May 1975)—these debates should not be permitted to overshadow intellectual contributions. If DH is to continue to thrive, it must balance the necessity of critical reflection with the productive work of scholarship, resisting the paralysing temptation of endless introspection and boundary-policing.

It is possible that *more* of the boundary-drawing, disciplinary navel-gazing would provide protections from interdisciplinarity being privileged overzealously without consideration of the consequences for how disciplines are perceived and how their constituents cohere (Sugimoto and Weingart 2015, 789). Disciplines provide the frameworks necessary for intellectual engagement and exchange, and in emerging disciplines, interrogating what constitutes excellence, and who benefits or suffers under such determinations, is vital to the consolidation and evolution of theory and practice.

Perhaps none of this matters, that the centuries-old age of disciplinarity is coming to an end, with scholars reverting to the idea of trans-applicable subject expertise in the face of a few remaining pockets of disciplinary resistance. Or perhaps the age of disciplinarity is only about to begin, and the reaction against persistent rumination on DH or any other emergent field reflects our institutes of higher education, where change to a formation as fundamental as discipline must be a slow and considered process.

The rise of generative AI really could serve as a clarifying moment for DH. As attention shifts toward AI's potential to disrupt the humanities—and indeed, humanity—DH can leverage established expertise in critically engaging with technology, providing opportunity to reaffirm its relevance. While analysing literary style through statistics may not have been sufficient justification of the value of the digital humanities—be that in the imagination of the public or wider scholarly community—large language models, which do a lot of the things DH scholars have been experimenting with and writing about for a long time, have certainly gotten everyone talking about the relationship between language, human expression, and computers. The challenge, then, is to use the energy spent on existential debates more constructively, doing the things that DH does best, rather than just talking about what those things might or should ideally be.

DH IS SOMETHING

Whatever the repercussions for the academy at large, however exhausted the "what is/are DH?" debate might be, there remain strong epistemological and practical reasons for engaging with this essential question. In the frank words of Max Kemman, we need to know if research in this domain should be considered "a valuable contribution or as nonsense" (Kemman 2017). That is essentially what this all comes down to: is there a point to digital humanities, or is it all just an excuse for bad scholars and critics to justify their existence without doing any actual scholarship or criticism? If you cannot read and write well enough, then just play with some digital tools and technologies.

Defining DH matters because DH is something, and if we are to figure out what to do with it, or indeed, what it is doing to us, then we need to establish the state-of-the-field as it exists in the present moment, where it has come from and where it might be going, and how it impacts upon the wider arts and humanities. Whether one likes it or not, the digital humanities exist, they are, as Stephen Ramsay so famously put it, much more than some airy Lyceum:

> Digital Humanities is not some airy Lyceum. It is a series of concrete instantiations involving money, students, funding agencies, big schools, little schools, programs, curricula, old guards, new guards, gatekeepers, and prestige. It might be more than these things, but it cannot not be these things.
>
> (Ramsay 2013, 240)

Faced with this reality, with the rise of DH and all the methodological and material appeal which has made it so attractive to institutions and people, it is intellectually irresponsible to disengage entirely with the act of defining, both now and into the future. We do not need to agree on what good DH entails, but anyone who pretends to see value in it, to teach it, to participate in its continued growth, should also feel obligated to scrutinise and refine the ontology of that in which they are active participants. That is why we should always continue to define and redefine DH, so that it might remain a nexus, but one with thoughtful, fluid boundaries, but also community-driven disciplinary realities that should not be ignored by those within and outside the discipline.

T. S. Eliot once wrote that culture, if it is to flourish, requires tension, that it needs to be "a constellation of cultures" with "friction between its parts" (Eliot 1949, 58). Whether one labels this particular disciplinary culture as "nexus" or "constellation," the synthesis between Fitzpatrick and Eliot is clear: DH, like any culture, is what emerges from friction. We can think of DH as a collision of others, as the disciplinary culture which remains when the humanities and computer sciences coalesce with intention. This sense of *intention* should be privileged in any consideration of the digital humanities: knowledge does not just happen; it is produced through processes of great intention, and scholars who do DH well do it well because they have concluded that a computer-assisted approach is optimal in solving the problems which they encounter. The digital humanities are not when any humanities scholar uses a computer; they are when scholars and practitioners, lecturers, professors, artists, librarians, archivists, programmers, physicists, technicians, come together to achieve something of *scholarly value*. That their perspectives have been formed across a myriad of disciplinary cultures will inevitably lead to friction, and that friction, the distillation of such essential difference, leads into something composite. That something is DH.

The digital humanities are a collection of fields which remain interconnected by two prevailing disciplinary practices: the application of sophisticated computational methods to arts and humanities research, and/or the critical examination of technology from a humanities perspective. In both instances, intention is vital: in the first, the application of technology to arts and humanities research, one must *need* the computer to answer their research question, and it should be blindingly clear what the computational technique brings; in the second instance, the critical examination of technology, the purpose should be to develop a greater understanding of the human condition as mediated through computing. Coining the term around the turn of the century, Schreibman, Siemens, and Unsworth described digital humanities in similar terms, as "using information technology to illuminate the human record, and bringing an understanding of the human record to bear on the development and use of information technology" (Schreibman et al. 2004, xxiii).

What such work looks like in practice will be explained throughout this book (and that really is the purpose of this book), but for now it is worth remembering that DH is all about using computers to do something of intellectual value, it is about detecting the latent semantic patterns in a large set of texts or visualising a network of correspondence. It is not posting to social media or sending emails. Readers who remain unconvinced of the difference between computing as something which is essential to certain kinds of macro-analytical research and computing as it exists as an everyday tool might be reading the wrong book. Posting to Instagram and big data analysis, using word embeddings to analyse literature or posing a query to ChatGPT, are just not the same thing.

While the depictions of the digital humanities as both computer-assisted analysis and cultural criticism of the digital seem markedly opposed, they are both, as Fitzpatrick puts it, the humanities, done digitally, just at opposite ends of a broad technical spectrum. Whether one is concerned with DH as computer-assisted method or DH as the cultural criticism of computation, those engaged in the field must possess a deep appreciation of the humanities *and* digital technologies. Whether one wishes to use the computer to assist in reading or wants to critique the computer in culture, it is important to understand both the processes of reading and machines.

It is true to state that "all scholars now use digital practices to some degree" (Mullen 2013, 238), but it is hugely reductive to suggest that computer-assisted analytics and cultural criticism of machines, are the same as just using a computer. All scholars read, but it would be absurd to suggest they are literary critics; most scholars probably use Google Maps, but that does not make them geographers. It is not remarkable that scholars across all disciplines use computers. The question is *how* they are using them? How are they analysing cultural materials? How are they critiquing computers in culture and society? It is widely inaccurate to suggest, as Lincoln Mullen does, that there are only "a few steps" between searching Word documents, using Zotero and text mining (Mullen 2013, 237). To conflate the use of tools like Word and Zotero, that are designed for everyday productivity, with text mining, certainly, of the sophisticated, publishable sort, epitomises the lack of understanding which routinely belittles this field. If the digital humanities are the humanities, done digitally, then suggesting that using Word and Zotero is DH is suggesting that the humanities is just reading and typing. It is a lazy characterisation.

There are very few parallels which can be drawn between the everyday use of a familiar computer programme such as Microsoft Word and sophisticated text mining techniques used to achieve hugely impressive intellectual feats in the quantitative analysis of complex lexical, syntactical and semantic phenomena like style, gender, sentiment and theme. Such techniques are "opening new possibilities for exploring challenging questions at the heart of some of the most pressing contemporary cultural and social issues" (Nguyen et al. 2019).

In the late-eighties, John Burrows published *Computation into Criticism: A Study of Jane Austen's Novels and an Experiment in Method* (1987), a ground-breaking text in which the author uses computational techniques to analyse the distribution of words in Jane Austen's works, producing a series of major findings on matters such as character interrelationships and dialogue. The following year, in 1988, the Women Writers Project received funding from the National Endowment for the Humanities, thus beginning several decade's worth of digitisation leading to one of the finest digital scholarly resources in existence. The nineties saw the emergence of the Text Encoding Initiative (Cummings 2008) a new-dominant encoding standard used to transform data from the arts and humanities into electronic form. Subsequent decades saw the emergence of an increasing number of resources, projects and methodologies, and now, at this moment in the emergence of DH, we are privileged to exist in an era of scholarship where computers are being used to ask and re-interrogate all sorts of questions and answers. In recent years, computational analysis has led to major discoveries in areas such as authorial gender signals (Rybicki 2016), the social networks that exist both in and around literature genre and plot (Koeser and Croxall 2013; Reagan et al. 2016; Underwood 2016; "Nation, Genre & Gender," n.d.), while a myriad of digital platforms have been used to create resources which offer functions beyond that of what can be accomplished on the page (O'Sullivan 2018a). None of these projects can be described as being only "a few steps" from using Microsoft Word.

Beyond such analytical projects, there is theory, the self-reflective ways in which the critical perspectives of the arts and humanities are brought to bear on the digital as the dominant mode of cultural production and reception in the age of information. In her influential essay on the topic, Johanna Drucker notes that the "cultural authority of digital technology is still claimed by the fields that design the platforms and protocols on which we work" (Drucker

2012) and that DH can and should be seen as the space where scholars and practitioners from the arts and humanities deliberately intervene in the design, development and criticism of digital systems, so central to contemporary culture and everyday life. We can see from all of this that in the digital humanities, some projects are technical, others are not, some are analytical, and others are not. But all these projects and activities are intellectually valuable, and they require advanced understanding of computers and our relationship to such digital technologies.

And whether technical or theoretical, such work, unlike, say, the use of Word as the *de facto* tool for typing up documents (or increasingly, the use of ChatGPT to autogenerate the content), is *intentional*—methodologically and critically—in the ways in which it applies or treats the computer is either an essential element of method or the primary cultural object of study.

WHEN ARE THE HUMANITIES, DIGITAL?

In the introduction to their 2015 primer on the digital humanities, Eileen Gardiner and Ronald G. Musto conclude with a series of questions (Gardiner and Musto 2015, 2). Do we now, ten years later, have answers to those questions?

"Are they [the digital humanities] a series of practical approaches?" Yes, a major aspect of DH involves applying the practical affordances of modern computing to the arts and humanities so that we can conduct forms of research previously beyond our own intrinsic mental capacities. Busa recognised this from the very beginning, remarking that even the seemingly trivial tasks of text processing play an important scientific role in conducting studies once considered infeasible (Busa 1980, 87).

"Are they a distinct discipline with its own set of standards, distinguished researchers, hierarchies and rules of engagement?" Certainly, as evidenced by the last three-or-so decades of professionalisation, wherein numerous dedicated journals, conferences and other community-driven initiatives have emerged. Seasoned members of this community know each other, newcomers know who they would like to know, and it is becoming increasingly clear what good and bad DH looks like.

"Or even more far-reaching, is the term *digital humanities* a redundancy? That is, are the humanities, like all contemporary scientific research and teaching, already digital to all important extents and purposes?" No, there is a marked difference between something that is just digital, and the explicit, conscious pursuit of something that may be considered to belong to the scholarly community of praxis which identifies as digital humanities.

In addition, DH is a space where further methodological advances are increasingly being made and their insights developed and evaluated in an environment that is constantly changing. The idea that all humanities scholars can or will soon be able to do everything their colleagues in DH can do is an exaggeration of most people's competency with computers, even the new generation of "digital natives," who are far more comfortable with intuitive interfaces and limited, out-of-the-box tools. DH will never "just be" humanities, because the digital part will continue to progress, offering an increasing number of possibilities to the humanities, each one requiring a different kind of expertise. DH will always be slightly other, because it will be thinking *intentionally* about the digital element, expanding and reflecting upon its possibilities and capacities. If the age of generative AI has taught us anything, it is that the current methodology is not the ultimate methodology.

Busa's story serves as a useful parable for much of what has been discussed in this chapter. Measured by the technical standards of today, the *Index Thomisticus* is little more than a rudimentary tool that allows text files to be searched. But Busa's project was truly revolutionary in that it showed how computers could hold *both* utilitarian *and* interpretive value for the humanities, not with "computers" as they are now considered, but rather, with punched card machinery. It is significant that Busa did not know what type of machinery he would need, but that he had thought very *consciously* about the need for "some type" and that he *understood*, as evidenced throughout his writings on the project both before and after its completion, the potential of what such machinery would offer (Busa 1980, 83). In one sense, the *Index* is just about efficiency, about taking an established technique involving the "ancient method" of handwritten index cards, and vastly improving its critical efficacy, liberating scholars who came after its completion to expend more energy analysing the greater volumes of linguistic evidence to which they had immediate access, allowing a redistribution of the balance of labour in favour of the interpretive aspects of research, and offering a resource for future analysis. The *Index* might be seen as a dataset upon which computer-assisted analyses were based, or as an early example of what new insights can be achieved from counting words at scale. Is it a reminder that, in the current age where we increasingly fetishise algorithmic complexity, considerable insight can be achieved with very little computation or number-crunching of the mathematical sort? If he were around today, would Busa be considered a scholar of DH's analytical school, or would he be a resource builder? Is the *Index* an act of computational analytics or remediation, or is it both?

However one views the *Index Thomisticus*, we know it is DH, because it could not have existed unless its stakeholders recognised the immense potential for using computers to do something of value in the arts and humanities. Computers were already doing things before Busa decided to use them in his work, just as literary scholars and historians had been analysing texts long before anyone decided to do so using digital techniques. The difference between DH and its others lies in the value that the computer brings to the task of answering particular questions, however big or small they might be. Defining a discipline in such terms is difficult, because notions like value and intention can be transient and partisan. What is considered an intentional application of a computer, yielding valuable results based on a true understanding of the methods applied, will differ across the arts and humanities, and as such, there will always be a measure of fluidity in any construction of the digital humanities. But if one considers any such endeavours in the context of these principles, then one will know DH when one sees it. Indeed, how scholars, institutions and the public define the digital humanities matters less than how it operates: what matters is what DH does.

RECOMMENDED READING

Gardiner, Eileen, and Ronald G. Musto. 2015. *The Digital Humanities: A Primer for Students and Scholars*. Cambridge University Press.

Hammond, Adam. 2016. *Literature in the Digital Age: An Introduction*. New York: Cambridge University Press.

McCarty, Willard. 2005. *Humanities Computing*. Palgrave Macmillan.

Nyhan, Julianne, and Andrew Flinn. 2016. *Computation and the Humanities: Towards an Oral History of Digital Humanities*. Springer.

O'Sullivan, James. 2023. *The Bloomsbury Handbook to the Digital Humanities*. Bloomsbury Academic.

Terras, Melissa, Julianne Nyhan, and Edward Vanhoutte, eds. 2013. *Defining Digital Humanities: A Reader*. Ashgate.

Underwood, Ted. *The Stone and the Shell* (blog). https://tedunderwood.com/

NOTES

1 A CD-ROM was circulated in the early nineties, before Enrique Alarcón and Eduardo Bernot brought the Index to the web in 2005: www.corpusthomisticum.org/it/index.age

2 It should be noted that the Society of Jesus has long been seen as one of Catholicism's more "radical" orders, relatively liberal in their leanings and often credited with aiding scientific progression (Wright 2004). Presented in such a light, it is perhaps unsurprising that Roberto Busa was a Jesuit.

3 See, for example, work by Dalbello (2011), Jones (2013), Nyhan and Flinn (2016a), Sula and Hill (2017), and Fiormonte and del Rio Riande (2023).

4 In 2011, Stanford University hosted *Digital Humanities*, the major annual gathering of DH scholars. The theme for DH2011 was "The Big Tent."

5 One can imagine that many commentators are currently working on "What is Artificial Intelligence and What's It Doing in English Departments?" variants.

REFERENCES

Black, Edwin. 2001. *IBM and the Holocaust*. Crown Publishing Group.

Burrows, J. F. 1987. *Computation into Criticism: A Study of Jane Austen's Novels and an Experiment in Method*. Clarendon Press.

Busa, Roberto. 1980. "The Annals of Humanities Computing: The Index Thomisticus." *Computers and the Humanities* 14 (2): 83–90.

Cain, Jeffrey. 2001. "On the Crisis of Self-Definition in English Studies." *Rocky Mountain Review of Language and Literature* 55 (1): 83–92. doi:10.2307/1348156

Cordell, Ryan. 2016. "How Not to Teach Digital Humanities." In *Debates in the Digital Humanities 2016*, edited by Matthew K. Gold and Lauren F. Klein. University of Minnesota Press. https://dhdebates.gc.cuny.edu/read/untitled/section/31326090-9c70-4c0a-b2b7-74361582977e#ch36

Cummings, James. 2008. "The Text Encoding Initiative and the Study of Literature." In *A Companion to Digital Literary Studies*, edited by Susan Schreibman and Ray Siemens. Blackwell. https://companions.digitalhumanities.org/DLS/?chapter=content/9781405148641_chapter_25.html

Dalbello, Marija. 2011. "A Genealogy of Digital Humanities." *Journal of Documentation* 67 (3): 480–506. doi:10.1108/00220411111124550

Dombrowski, Quinn. 2019. "*Technical Enough*." https://digitalhumanities.stanford.edu/technical-enough

Drucker, Johanna. 2012. "Humanistic Theory and Digital Scholarship." In *Debates in the Digital Humanities*, edited by Matthew K. Gold. University of Minnesota Press.

Drucker, Johanna. 2023. "Normative Digital Humanities." In *The Bloomsbury Handbook to the Digital Humanities*, edited by James O'Sullivan, 7–17. London: Bloomsbury Academic.

Eliot, T. S. 1949. *Notes Towards the Definition of Culture*. Harcourt, Brace.

Fiormonte, Domenico, and Gimena del Rio Riande. 2023. "The Peripheries and Epistemic Margins of Digital Humanities." In *The Bloomsbury Handbook to the Digital Humanities*, edited by James O'Sullivan, 19–28. London: Bloomsbury Academic. doi:10.5281/zenodo.8075239

Fitzpatrick, Kathleen. 2010. "Reporting from the Digital Humanities 2010 Conference." *The Chronicle of Higher Education: ProfHacker* (blog). July 13, 2010. www.chronicle.com/blogs/profhacker/reporting-from-the-digital-humanities-2010-conference/25473

Fitzpatrick, Kathleen. 2012. "The Humanities, Done Digitally." In *Debates in the Digital Humanities*, edited by Matthew K. Gold. University of Minnesota Press.

Gardiner, Eileen, and Ronald G. Musto. 2015. *The Digital Humanities: A Primer for Students and Scholars*. Cambridge University Press.

Gold, Matthew K., ed. 2012a. *Debates in the Digital Humanities*. University of Minnesota Press. https://dhdebates.gc.cuny.edu/projects/debates-in-the-digital-humanities

Gold, Matthew K., ed. 2012b. "The Digital Humanities Moment." In *Debates in the Digital Humanities*, edited by Matthew K. Gold. University of Minnesota Press.

Gold, Matthew K., and Lauren F. Klein, eds. 2016. *Debates in the Digital Humanities 2016*. University of Minnesota Press. https://dhdebates.gc.cuny.edu/projects/debates-in-the-digital-humanities-2016

Gold, Matthew K., and Lauren F. Klein, eds. 2019. *Debates in the Digital Humanities 2019*. University of Minnesota Press. https://dhdebates.gc.cuny.edu/projects/debates-in-the-digital-humanities-2019

Hewson, Mark. 2018. "The Debate with Method in the History of Literary Studies." *Comparative Literature Studies* 55 (1): 23–46. doi:10.5325/complitstudies.55.1.0023

Hockey, Susan. 2004. "The History of Humanities Computing." In *A Companion to Digital Humanities*, edited by Susan Schreibman, Ray Siemens, and John Unsworth. Blackwell. https://companions.digitalhumanities.org/DH/?chapter=content/9781405103213_chapter_1.html

Jones, Steven E. 2013. *The Emergence of the Digital Humanities*. Routledge.

Jones, Steven E. 2016. *Roberto Busa, S. J., and the Emergence of Humanities Computing: The Priest and the Punched Cards*. Routledge.

Kemman, Max. 2017. "Why Do We Need a Definition of DH?" *Max Kemman* (blog). 2017. https://web.archive.org/web/20170830032147/http://www.maxkemman.nl/2017/06/why-do-we-need-a-definition-of-dh/

Kirschenbaum, Matthew. 2012a. "Digital Humanities As/Is a Tactical Term." In *Debates in the Digital Humanities*, edited by Matthew K. Gold. University of Minnesota Press. https://dhdebates.gc.cuny.edu/read/untitled-88c11800-9446-469b-a3be-3fdb36bfbd1e/section/c0b0a8ee-95f0-4a9c-9451-e8ad168e3db5

Kirschenbaum, Matthew. 2012b. "What Is Digital Humanities and What's It Doing in English Departments?" In *Debates in the Digital Humanities*, edited by Matthew K. Gold. University of Minnesota Press. https://dhdebates.gc.cuny.edu/read/untitled-88c11800-9446-469b-3be-3fdb36bfbd1e/section/f5640d43-b8eb-4d49-bc4b-eb31a16f3d06

Kirschenbaum, Matthew. 2014. "What Is 'Digital Humanities,' and Why Are They Saying Such Terrible Things about It?" *Differences* 25 (1): 46–63.

Koeser, Rebecca Sutton, and Brian Croxall. 2013. "Networking the Belfast Group through the Automated Semantic Enhancement of Existing Digital Content." *Journal of Digital Humanities* 2 (3). http://journalofdigitalhumanities.org/2-3/networking-the-belfast-group-through-the-automated-semantic-enhancement-of-existing-digital-content/

Liu, Alan. 2012. "Where Is Cultural Criticism in the Digital Humanities?" In *Debates in the Digital Humanities*, edited by Matthew K. Gold. University of Minnesota Press. https://liu.english.ucsb.edu/where-is-cultural-criticism-in-the-digital-humanities/.

Losh, Elizabeth, and Jacqueline Wernimont. 2019. *Bodies of Information: Intersectional Feminism and the Digital Humanities*. University of Minnesota Press.

May, Kenneth O. 1975. "What Is Good History and Who Should Do It?" *Historia Mathematica* 2: 449–455.

Mullen, Lincoln. 2013. "Digital Humanities Is a Spectrum, or 'We're All Digital Humanists Now'." In *Defining Digital Humanities*, edited by Melissa Terras, Julianne Nyhan, and Edward Vanhoutte, 237–238. Ashgate.

"Nation, Genre & Gender." n.d. www.nggprojectucd.ie/

Nguyen, Dong, Maria Liakata, Simon DeDeo, Jacob Eisenstein, David Mimno, Rebekah Tromble, and Jane Winters. 2019. "How We Do Things with Words: Analyzing Text as Social and Cultural Data." *arXiv*, July. http://arxiv.org/abs/1907.01468

Nyhan, Julianne, and Andrew Flinn. 2016a. *Computation and the Humanities: Towards an Oral History of Digital Humanities*. Springer.

Nyhan, Julianne, and Andrew Flinn. 2016b. "Hic Rhodus, Hic Salta: Tito Orlandi and Julianne Nyhan." In *Computation and the Humanities: Towards an Oral*

History of Digital Humanities, edited by Julianne Nyhan and Andrew Flinn, 75–86. Springer. doi:10.1007/978-3-319-20170-2_5

O'Sullivan, James. 2018a. "The Equivalence of Books: Monographs, Prestige, and the Rise of Edge Cases." *Convergence: The International Journal of Research into New Media Technologies* 24 (5): 494–503. doi:10.1177/1354856518780457

O'Sullivan, James. 2018b. "We Need to Talk about the Digital Humanities Job." *Talking Humanities*. https://cora.ucc.ie/handle/10468/6460

Parry, Dave. 2012. "The Digital Humanities or a Digital Humanism." In *Debates in the Digital Humanities*, edited by Matthew K. Gold. University of Minnesota Press. https://dhdebates.gc.cuny.edu/read/untitled-88c11800-9446-469b-a3be-3fdb36bfbd1e/section/c3127960-92ee-4b32-8b69-38f87aa2d9c5

Ramsay, Stephen. 2013. "Who's In and Who's Out." In *Defining Digital Humanities*, edited by Melissa Terras, Julianne Nyhan, and Edward Vanhoutte, 239–241. Ashgate.

Reagan, Andrew J., Lewis Mitchell, Dilan Kiley, Christopher M. Danforth, and Peter Sheridan Dodds. 2016. "The Emotional Arcs of Stories Are Dominated by Six Basic Shapes." *EPJ Data Science* 5 (1): 31. doi:10.1140/epjds/s13688-016-0093-1

Risam, Roopika. 2018. *New Digital Worlds: Postcolonial Digital Humanities in Theory, Praxis, and Pedagogy*. Evanston, IL: Northwestern University Press.

Risam, Roopika, and Kelly Baker Josephs. 2021. *The Digital Black Atlantic*. University of Minnesota Press.

Rockwell, Geoffrey, and Marco Passarotti. 2019. "The Index Thomisticus as a Big Data Project." *Umanistica Digitale* 5 (May). doi:10.6092/issn.2532-8816/8575

Rybicki, Jan. 2016. "Vive La Différence: Tracing the (Authorial) Gender Signal by Multivariate Analysis of Word Frequencies." *Digital Scholarship in the Humanities* 31 (4): 746–761. doi:10.1093/llc/fqv023

Schreibman, Susan, Ray Siemens, and John Unsworth. 2004. "The Digital Humanities and Humanities Computing: An Introduction." In *A Companion to Digital Humanities*, edited by Susan Schreibman, Ray Siemens, and John Unsworth. Blackwell. https://companions.digitalhumanities.org/DH/?chapter=content/9781405103213_intro.html

Spiro, Lisa. 2012. "'This Is Why We Fight': Defining the Values of the Digital Humanities." In *Debates in the Digital Humanities*, edited by Matthew K. Gold. Minneapolis: University of Minnesota Press. https://dhdebates.gc.cuny.edu/read/untitled-88c11800-9446-469b-3be-3fdb36bfbd1e/section/9e014167-688-43ab-8b12-0f6746095335

Stanley, Sarah. 2017. "Why Is Digital Humanities?" https://web.archive.org/web/20170621221508/http://scatherinestanley.us/2017/06/why-is-dh

Sugimoto, Cassidy R., and Scott Weingart. 2015. "The Kaleidoscope of Disciplinarity." *Journal of Documentation* 71 (4): 775–794.

Sula, Chris Alen, and Heather Hill. 2017. "The Early History of Digital Humanities." https://dh2017.adho.org/abstracts/347/347.pdf

Underwood, Ted. 2016. "The Life Cycles of Genres." *Journal of Cultural Analytics*. doi:10.22148/16.005

Underwood, Ted. 2017. "Digital Humanities as a Semi-Normal Thing." *The Stone and the Shell* (blog). 2017. https://tedunderwood.com/2017/03/30/digital-humanities-as-a-semi-normal-thing/

Underwood, Ted. 2019. "Digital Humanities as a Semi-Normal Thing." In *Debates in the Digital Humanities*, edited by Matthew K. Gold and Lauren F. Klein, 96–98. University of Minnesota Press. doi:10.5749/j.ctvg251hk.13

Unsworth, John. 2002. "What Is Humanities Computing and What Is Not?" http://computerphilologie.uni-muenchen.de/jg02/unsworth.html

Woods, Susanne. 1994. "Recovering the Past, Discovering the Future: The Brown University Women Writers Project." *South Central Review* 11 (2): 17–23. doi:10.2307/3189986

Wright, Jonathan. 2004. *God's Soldiers: Adventure, Politics, Intrigue, and Power: A History of the Jesuits*. Doubleday.

2

DH AS METHODS, THEORY OR SHARING

In January 2011, thousands of scholars descended on Los Angeles as the city played host to the Modern Language Association's annual convention. The "what is DH?" debate was very much in vogue, and many of those arriving in L.A. were excited by the prospect of the "History and Future of Digital Humanities" panel featuring contributions from a cohort of the field's most recognisable names: Kathleen Fitzpatrick, Alan Liu, Tara McPherson, Kathy Harris, Bethany Nowviskie, Brett Bobley, and Stephen Ramsay. Each speaker was given three minutes to offer a position paper on the topic of concern, a distinctly brief amount of time considering the reaction that the soon-to-be-infamous Ramsay was able to generate with his position paper, "Who's In and Who's Out." In a later republication of the piece, Ramsay quips: "Boy, did this get me in trouble" (Ramsay 2013b, 241).

The source of animosity was his contention that the ability to write computer code is essential to any scholar wishing to be counted among the true acolytes of DH: "Do you have to know how to code? I'm a tenured professor of digital humanities and I

DOI: 10.4324/9781351203395-2

say 'yes'" (Ramsay 2013b, 240). While much of the fallout was centred on that one adversarial remark, Ramsay's argument is far more nuanced than is often credited. He does not think that all DH scholars should be software developers, but that they should be *building* something. What constitutes "building" can be "highly expansive" in definition, but "if you are not making anything, you are not … a digital humanist" (Ramsay 2013b, 241). In a subsequent essay, Ramsay clarified his position, outlining what such "building" might entail: visualisation, mapping, and encoding are examples of the types of acts of production which Ramsay sees as separating the *digital* humanities from the humanities. Activity of this sort, building things using technology is a "process of creation" which "yields insights that are difficult to acquire otherwise" (Ramsay 2013a, 244–245). According to Ramsay, all the "big names" in DH have grease under their fingernails (Ramsay 2013a, 245).

In his later essay, Ramsay invokes the figure of Alan Liu, who, in 1994, started a website for humanities research titled, "Voice of the Shuttle." Reflecting on the project back in the mid-nineties, Liu describes himself as a *bricoleur* (Liu 1996).[1] Most significantly developed by Claude Lévi-Strauss, the concept of bricolage formulates a dichotomy between the savage and scientific mind (1966). The scientific mind (the engineer) possesses the expertise to develop elegant, totalising solutions, whereas the savage (the *bricoleur*) is a craftsman, relying on existing resources or repurposing whatever might be at hand to get the job done. Liu's self-characterisation is that of a "technological savage," an "English professor and not a computer specialist" whose forays in the early Web might well appear "inexact, incomplete, inefficient, or worse" to a maestro (Liu 1996). Ramsay thinks Liu is being unkind to himself, that he is more than a *bricoleur* or a "bumbling hacker," that he is a builder in the truest sense, a true "crossover act" with the greasy fingernails to prove it (Ramsay 2013a, 245).

It is useful to think about the digital humanities in terms of *bricoleurs* and engineers. The DH *bricoleurs* are those who patch together whatever digital tools and resources might be available to achieve their technical ambitions, while the engineers design and construct their own code and algorithms. There are very few, if any, engineers, very few people capable of developing complete solutions without the need to draw from the endeavours of others. The engineer is something of a myth.[2] If it is true that only "a radical subset of the DH community knows how to code" (Ramsay 2013a, 245), then most DH scholars, even if "building things," are *bricoleurs*, masters of a craft that might benefit from some programming skills, but certainly, requires an advanced understanding of how existing techniques, technical libraries and frameworks might be applied to any given problem.

The *bricoleur* should not be seen as less than the engineer, because there is great skill and creativity required in acts of perverse engineering, in taking tools and techniques developed for some other purpose and using them to achieve new meanings in domains beyond those for which they are intended. The digital humanities are full of *bricoleurs* who have used existing tools and platforms to achieve some purpose other than that for which such systems were originally developed. Much like postmodern artistic movements like Dadaism relied on everyday, found objects or so-called ready-mades, the DH *bricoleur* relies on found technologies,[3] existing tools and platforms—which may or may not have been designed with DH users in mind—to do their digital work. The figure of the engineer is a useful aspiration, as practitioners in this space should never stop striving for the (however mythical) idealised version of any digital tool, technique, or resource. But there is no doubt that the digital humanities have been built by *bricoleurs*, by elegant patchwork and hacking.

Ultimately, however one sees *bricoleurs* and engineers, the hallmark of the DH scholar, according to Ramsay, is that they are *makers*. Bricolage is itself an act of interpretation, and the found technologies of the *bricoleur* operate as prisms through which certain aspects of a research question might be magnified, tabulated, and reconsidered. Take, for example, the business of text encoding, which could be narrowly construed as little more than the addition of tags to a text for the purposes of structuring content, when it is in fact a highly interpretive process which involves embedding an expert reader's critical observations into the paratextual body of a work. Ramsay argues that the value in DH is all in the making, because making allows for a different sort of understanding than reading: "Media studies, game studies, critical code studies, and various other disciplines have brought wonderful new things to humanistic study, but I will say (at my peril) that none of these represent as radical a shift as the move from reading to making" (Ramsay 2013a, 244). Whether or not one's approach to text encoding is technically ideal, encoding of any sort leads to intimacy with a text and its materiality that will allow for a different sort of understanding than reading alone.

Sitting down to "tag" a document using something like XML, a markup language for structuring data, forces whoever is doing the work to think explicitly about the formal and interpretative aspects of their content. If one is going to mark-up a piece of text, they need to think formally about how that text is or should be structured, what content should be given additional context, and what, in their interpretation, is worth tagging. Marking up a page of text is very different to reading that page, in that the former requires active participation in how that page, in its digital form, will be represented. It is a very different kind of engagement that naturally produces a different kind of understanding on the part of the maker.

If there is something different, something valuable in making things, why did Stephen Ramsay get into so much trouble for arguing that digital humanities scholars should all be coders, or at the very least, that they should be building? The problem with Ramsay's vision for the digital humanities is that it leaves little room for theorists, those who have much to offer on the nature of computers in culture, but really, are not all that interested in being builders themselves. And as we will see in this chapter, the digital humanities, and indeed, other disciplines and society-at-large, really needs these people as well. Having them in the digital humanities, where they can work with and through the builders, seems like a reasonable way to advance the field in desirable directions. It may seem surprising, but despite years of well-reasoned (and sometimes heated) arguments, the DH as analytical versus theoretical debate is far from being resolved: some people think DH is all about making, others disagree. Just when it seemed as though DH had settled on some kind of compromise, along came cultural analytics and computational humanities as "anti-theory" monikers.

Of course, it never really is just one or the other: theory provides the critical frameworks necessary to interrogate the cultural, social, and ethical dimensions of digital tools and methods, while technical making embodies the practice of creation, offering tangible outputs that ground theoretical inquiry in real-world application. These two approaches to scholarship usually (though not always) function in tandem, with critical perspectives shaping the design and implementation of methodologies and tools, technical practice informing and challenging theoretical assumptions, before theory comes back in for the interpretation. But Ramsay's argument is still useful, because it emphasises the value in building.

And the age of machine learning and generative AI has given Ramsay's essay renewed significance. Building, making—all the technical stuff like forming datasets and training models—provides a hands-on understanding of AI's capabilities and limitations, essential for anyone who wishes to do a theoretical interrogation of how these technologies shape knowledge production and cultural meaning. Critiquing how, say, large language models like ChatGPT are impacting writing requires a comprehensive understanding of technical concepts like transformers and inference mechanisms—how can the ways in which these models fundamentally reshape writing be analysed without grasping the mechanics of how these systems generate text, how they parse input and predict language patterns? You need the grease under the fingernails.

Engaging with the "what is and what is not DH" debate is not about excluding anyone, it is about seeing what is privileged, what is missing, what the digital turn in the arts and humanities has achieved, and how it has failed. Disciplinarity is only a useful concept when it is used as a framework for the interrogation of real intellectual practices, things that people are doing in research and education. Engaging in such debates seems far more valuable than simply throwing one's hands up and saying that all this "navel gazing" does not matter. If the project of DH is to advance, we need to keep enquiring as to what DH means, what excellence looks like, why we think it worth doing instead of "just" computer science or "just" the humanities.

But it need not all be navel gazing. The value in disciplinarity is not in prescriptive meta-discussions, but in facilitating more descriptive explorations, identifying those tangible accomplishments which construct and illustrate some sense of what a field, or amalgam of several fields, might entail. Or, as it is more eloquently put by Matthew Kirschenbaum: "there is one thing that digital humanities ineluctably is: digital humanities is work, somebody's work, somewhere, some thing, always. We know how to talk about work. So let's talk about this work, in action, this actually existing work" (Kirschenbaum 2014, 61). As Chapter 1 concludes, what matters is what we do—so what do we do when we do DH?[4]

DH AS METHOD

Around the end of the twelfth and beginning of the thirteenth centuries, a major cultural transformation began to take shape in Europe: the quantification of all things started to become something of an obsession. By the sixteenth century, in order for reality to be considered such it had to be measurable (Crosby 1997, 238). Such an attitude to knowing is now dominant worldwide. It is unsurprising that instrumental measurement finally found its way into the arts and humanities, and the application of computational methods to the analysis of cultural materials is now one of the major forms of DH. From a methodological perspective, the major difference between the digital humanities and the wider arts and humanities is the application of computer-assisted techniques to cultural criticism, what is typically referred to as "cultural analytics," "distant reading," or "macro-analysis" (Jockers 2013). This strand of the digital humanities is all about the empirical study of culture, about using computational, statistical, big data methods to analyse documentary materials. For example, using statistics to determine whether Shakespeare was in fact a singular genius who composed all his works alone, without collaborators, is a typical example what an empirical analysis of culture might look like.

For many, this type of DH, using computers to statistically analyse cultural data, is the "real" DH. While commentators outside the community tend to attack DH in all its forms, the cold civil war within the digital humanities is between the "practitioners" and the "theorists," those who use computers for statistical analysis, and those who do everything else, be that cultural critique, sharing, or basically anything that is not computational analytics. Geoffrey Rockwell believes such divisions exist because there is a "residual fear" of theory in the digital humanities "because many digital humanists fled theory for application and because poor theory can be totalizing in a way we fear will delegitimize all the makings we struggled with in that 'gotcha' sort of way" (Jockers 2013, 249).

Thankfully, much of this has been sorted out, and the computational humanities people do computational humanities and have their own conferences and journals, and the broader digital humanities people have their own conferences and journals, and some people oscillate between both camps.

Academic squabbles aside, the computer-assisted analytical DH camp—the computational humanities and cultural analytics camp—is a big camp that remains unwaveringly central to the digital humanities. This is because the instrumental, critical value of using computational methods to address research questions in the arts and humanities has been convincingly demonstrated.

Cultural analytics allows scholars to go beyond the limitations of human perception, to ask questions of culture at scale. If a reader wants to understand the intricacies of a single text, they can go ahead and read the material in question and form an opinion. If they want to identify the common trends and patterns in hundreds, thousands, even millions of texts, they are probably going to need some help from a computer. Of course, one text can also benefit from computer-assisted analysis, as statistical analyses of texts, whether few or many, often reveals latent semantic patterns that unassisted human readers tend to miss.

Cultural analytics, computational humanities, distant reading—whatever you want to call it—advocates using approaches from the computer sciences, techniques from text mining and natural language processing, machine learning and artificial intelligence, to analyse cultural materials.

By analysing 15,000 book reviews from the *Sunday Book Review* and *The New York Times*, Andrew Piper and Richard

Jean So show how male and female authors are treated differently by critics, in that women writers are still seen as more sentimental, while men are typically defined by their interests in science and politics (Piper and So 2016). In taking such a large volume of reviews from two influential publications, Piper and So use data analysis to prove beyond doubt that critical biases regarding gender persist within the culturally significant business of book reviewing. Such a finding might not exactly come as a revelation to some but knowing something and providing empirical proof are two entirely different matters in an age in which quantitative evidence is increasingly fetishised. If one is to convince certain audiences of their perspective, particularly on matters of cultural bias, it really is necessary to demonstrate quantitative evidence.

Of course, just because something can be analysed using computers does not mean it should be analysed using computers. The use of computational techniques to study associations between gender, word usage, narrative and wider cultural contexts can be problematic when methodological limitations only serve to reify pre-existing dichotomies (Weidman and O'Sullivan 2018; O'Sullivan 2017). Furthermore, computational approaches to cultural criticism often rely on datasets in which women have been effaced. As Laura Mandell reminds us, even "in the absolute biggest datasets, the number of women is dwarfed in comparison to every man who ever wrote" (Mandell 2016, 520). In truth, there is something dangerously masculinist about the "greasy fingernails" slant of the discourse which surrounds computational work in the humanities. As will be discussed in Chapter 6, there are deep issues in how DH can sometimes exude a "boys with toys" mentality, or worse still, slip into a form of reactive misogyny. One must proceed carefully before providing empirical "proof" of anything to do with sensitive matters such as gender.

Of course, it is not just gender and its place in literature that has been subject to computer-assisted analysis, nor is it just in matters linguistic that such techniques have proved transformative. Computational techniques have yielded similarly fruitful analyses across a range of topics in the arts and humanities (as catalogued in Chapter 3); the key takeaway here is that a big part of DH is using data analytics to discover something about culture that might otherwise have been missed or be difficult to assert when using "unassisted" approaches to criticism and interpretation.

DH AS THEORY

Software is eating the world. We need the digital humanities for the very reasons its detractors cite when they argue that scientification is consuming the humanities. Indeed, all aspects of life, public and private, are now mediated through software systems that are being designed, developed and controlled by an increasingly small number of commercial entities. To say that computation has no place in the humanities, and vice versa, is to cede control of *everything* to those who control the software that mediates *everything*. The digital humanities can, in many ways, be accused of advancing the neoliberal agenda, but it is also a space in which one of the most potent instruments that has been appropriated by late capitalism can be resisted.

Our present age is one in which we can simply no longer afford to keep the sciences and the humanities apart. The danger in this position is that the former tends to swallow the latter, as institutions and policymakers tend to privilege the so-called STEM (science, technology, engineering, and mathematics) disciplines over the arts and humanities. The digital humanities, which *should* be rooted in cultural norms and disciplinary sensitivities of the wider arts and humanities, present an opportunity for scientific and humanistic perspectives to exist in interdisciplinary harmony.

A semi-popular poster which encapsulates this argument reads: "Science can tell you how to clone a *Tyrannosaurus rex*. Humanities can tell you why this might be a bad idea." Ted Underwood refers to this poster in his essay, "Why an Age of Machine Learning needs the Humanities":

> The real monster in our world is not a dinosaur we could avoid creating. It is human history, already broken loose, already ravenous and hard to predict. To understand it—to understand ourselves—we will need numbers as well as words. Humanists have a lot to

> contribute to this struggle, since we know the monster's past and understand its slipperiness better than anyone else.
>
> (Underwood 2018)

In other words, whether we like it or not, the sciences need the humanities, and vice versa. Johanna Drucker argues that the "cultural authority of digital technology" remains dominated by "quantitative, engineering, and computational sensibilities" and that the humanities can serve to redress these biases, providing "ways of thinking differently, otherwise, specific to the problems and precepts of interpretative knowing—partial, situated, enunciative, subjective, and performative" (Drucker 2012). As we continue to see advances in areas like artificial intelligence, when our very sense of fundamental constructs like "human" begins to muddy, the need for humanities-centric perspectives will only be enhanced. The digital humanities, a space for humanities scholars who have, at the very least, some passive interest in digital technologies, is precisely the site where such cultural authority should reside. Should such authority remain exclusively in the hands of the sciences and engineering, we are probably, if the world at present is anything to go by, going to end up with a lot of T. rexes.

Those who do theoretical work in DH are less concerned with the statistical analysis of documentary materials and are more concerned with thinking about the role of digital technologies in culture and society: how computation has transformed knowledge, meaning, communication, creativity, and expression. Drucker reminds us that "the role of humanities scholars is crucial in the production and interpretation of cultural materials" (Drucker 2012), and in a contemporary context, production invariably involves the digital. From such a perspective, digital humanities should be less concerned with statistical analyses, and more concerned with functioning as a space in which those digital platforms and instructions which increasingly mediate our cultures can be developed through more humanity-centric perspectives and processes. Drucker goes as far as to suggest that cultural analytics has never really achieved anything other than efficiency, enabling "easier access to primary materials, speed of comparison, searching, etc." (Drucker 2012). Drucker may well be trivialising the value of the statistical analysis discussed in this book, but the provocation is timely: do the digital humanities better serve the public through statistical analyses of cultural materials, or through the application of humanistic perspectives to digital technologies?

Of course, these two forms of DH can and do co-exist. Furthermore, regardless of whether one is using computers for the statistical analysis of cultural materials or being framed as the object of critique in a theoretical exploration of digital culture, both practices require an advanced understanding of computation, algorithms, data—the digital. Doing digital humanities well—statistical or theoretical—requires more than a passing interest in everyday desktop applications and web platforms. It really is time that the discipline moved beyond the tensions between analytics and theory, the builders and theorists, because both really do need each other. There are many research agendas and societal challenges in the arts and humanities that need the analytical capacity of computers; while the digital, so all-consuming in essence, cannot be allowed to extend its grip on culture and society without greater problematisation from the humanities.

It has been a decade or so since Rockwell claimed that the digital humanities are under-theorised. He attributed this to the field's need for practitioners, people who can *do* and *make* things with computers, coupled with a lingering fear of "being swallowed by postmodernisms" (Rockwell 2013, 249). People go into the digital humanities to get away from theory, to pursue new systems of knowledge creation based on building. That fear appears to have lessened over the past decade, which is positive, because building for building's sake achieves very little. The digital humanities are now (relatively) full of theory, practices which might be classified as "media studies," but still turn up at digital humanities conferences and gatherings, and in journals and syllabi (see Weingart and Eichmann-Kalwara 2017). The digital humanities now include the critical appreciation of born-digital electronic literature and videogames (Jones 2015; Rettberg 2016), postcolonial DH (Risam 2018), feminist DH (Ross 2018), labour (Boyles et al. 2018; Ross and Pilsch 2019), and other forms of cultural criticism which have previously "blocked" the digital humanities from becoming "a full partner" of the humanities (Liu 2012). And it is through such work that the "cultural authority of digital technology" is being reclaimed by the humanities.

DH AS SHARING

It is not unreasonable to suggest that, for all that has been transformed in the digital age, the greatest of revolutions has come through the Web (though generative AI feels like it is about to give it a run for its money). While it might seem so trivial to us now, when the sharing of content independent of location was first possible—specifically, when the Web became a more participatory space in the late nineties and early-to-mid noughties—*everything* changed. A lot of the early practitioners of DH recognised the Web as opportunity to transform the humanities beyond recognition, to democratise access to resources and knowledge, to offer materials and critical apparatus that were not constrained by the formal properties of print. Many of these scholars did not care about the statistical affordances of computers, or indeed, theorising the consequences for culture—they saw the Web and recognised an opportunity to *share*. For some DH scholars, such as Mark Sample, it is in sharing that the real value in the digital humanities is to be found:

> The promise of the digital is not in the way it allows us to ask new questions because of digital tools or because of new methodologies made possible by those tools. The promise is in the way the digital reshapes the representation, sharing, and discussion of knowledge.
>
> (Sample 2013, 256)

This perspective constructs the digital humanities as "public humanities," a universal set of principles intended to further widen public engagement with the humanities.[5] What could be more cultural and socially responsible than dedicating one's effort to the task of making the humanities more open and accessible?

There are many projects which illustrate the shape of DH when configured in the context of sharing, a sizeable portion of which might loosely be tied to the idea of digital publishing, using digital platforms of various sorts to facilitate new kinds of engagement between the creators and consumers of knowledge. In a comprehensive survey of this topic, Tobias Blanke, Elena Pierazzo and Peter A. Stokes conclude that many DH scholars and practitioners are solely occupied by "the new possibilities of digital publishing" (Blanke et al. 2014, 25), with developing and experimenting with new kinds of immersive materials and open models of dissemination.

Digital publishing can take many forms. At the most essential level, digital publishing can simply be about using online platforms to share research and ideas (Terras 2012; Morrison 2008). Thinking about how knowledge is shared should never be trivialised, as it allows individuals to take ownership of their research narratives. If scholars do not think carefully about the research story that they cultivate in public, they are allowing "Google, Yahoo, and Bing" to do it instead (Marshall 2015). In the age of surveillance capitalism and generative AI it has never been more important for scholars to think about how, why, and where they share. Taking the community-creating capacity of publishing seriously means cultivating habits and practices that establish and nourish scholarly publics which *enrich* relationships and *expand* scholarship at its root (O'Sullivan et al. 2016, 388).

The means through which the digital enables publics have never been more plentiful. Platforms like Omeka make it easy for scholars to create digital exhibitions of cultural heritage using Dublin Core, a popular metadata standard (Kucsma et al. 2010; Rath 2016), while endeavours such as the *Public Philosophy Journal* are pursuing new, more collegial systems of open review (O'Sullivan et al. 2016, 389). Scholars are using digital mapping to represent the incarceration of asylum seekers in visual acts of intervention;[6] and they are using platforms like Scalar to document the experience of early electronic literature before an entire generation of hypertextual fiction is lost to platform obsolescence (Grigar and Moulthrop 2015).

This is all greasy work, requiring scholars to delve into the unglamorous world of technical systems, metadata standards, and platform-specific constraints. It demands not only intellectual engagement but also a willingness to engage with the messy, practical realities of digital tools and infrastructures. Building digital publishing projects—whether through Omeka exhibitions or mapping platforms—is as much about storytelling as it is about preservation and intervention, giving its builders an intimate knowledge of the cultural content and its public reception that would not be achieved if consumed solely through close reading and individual attention.

DOING DIGITAL HUMANITIES

Towards the end of his foundational book, *Humanities Computing*, Willard McCarty concedes that his agenda for the field "remains far too generous in scope and includes far too many participants for me to give the whole a fair treatment" (McCarty 2005, 205). This may be the fate of any attempt to prescriptively define a discipline with any measure of granularity, and so the best that we can do is to state broad assumptions of typology and accept that there will always be exceptions to the rule. We should, of course, develop such typologies, but only when coupled with, and contextualised by, appreciation of actual scholarly practice, a recognition of what the constituents of the digital humanities are actually doing. Overly broad meta discussions of DH and vague statements about what it is and is not serve very little function beyond undergraduate classrooms and recruiting fairs.

We must accept that we are unlikely to ever agree upon a consistent agenda. DH can be constructed as being about methods, theory, or sharing just as literary studies examines differing epochs or relies on differing critical theories or disciplinary norms. There is no one history; there will be no one DH.

But if there can be one guiding principle, it should be this: *DH must be inherently digital in a way that brings value and meaning to the arts and humanities.* Doing the work of the humanities in the digital age where the ubiquitous presence of computing is an essential part of everyday life is not the same as doing DH. In the examples given throughout this book, the computer is epistemologically essential to the work being done—it is either instrumental to the analysis or it is the object of analysis. But what is certain is its presence. You do not go to a website and think, wow, this was done with a computer—when you see a classic novel reinterpreted using statistics, you do think, wow, this was done with a computer. The latter is DH.

Pointing to "exemplars" is always a risky business since they come in all shapes and sizes. The digital humanities cannot just be about *huge* projects, while it cannot be sustained on individual work alone. It cannot just be about infrastructure, about building capacity without any sense of why and how such capacity might contribute directly to the day-to-day research and pedagogical practices of scholars and educators. In fact, the digital humanities are inherently anti-infrastructure, in that everyone's DH looks different. Some think that tools are necessities, while others think that they are restrictive, black boxes. Some want to do "big" things with "lots" of data, others want to do "smaller" things with "one book." DH can be a major, grant-funded resource that makes available important cultural materials, but it can also be a short essay that uses a computational method to produce some new discovery, a little graph that indicates a massive trend. Some humanities scholars want to interpret rather than build and share, whereas others see building and sharing as acts of interpretation in themselves.

Stephen Ramsay reminds us that "the DH conference now draws a thousand people, that makes it something. It might be something for the wrong reasons, but it is something." We need only look at these gatherings to see what DH actually is, what it was, and what it might be. We do not all need to agree on what should and should not be included, but the first step in any such act of disciplinary disambiguation should be an understanding of what is being done in the present. Is that worth doing? Is there something else that would be more worthwhile? Does any of it matter? That seems as good a starting point as any.

There is no one DH, but it is important that those who do it, are fully aware of what they are doing and why. The digital part should be *essential* to the intellectual integrity of the work, rather than an addendum borne of expectation. Thankfully, work where the digital bit is essential and meaningful usually speaks for itself.

RECOMMENDED READING

Crompton, Constance, Richard J. Lane, and Ray Siemens, eds. 2016. *Doing Digital Humanities: Practice, Training, Research*. Routledge.

Crompton, Constance, Richard J. Lane, and Ray Siemens, eds. 2020. *Doing More Digital Humanities: Open Approaches to Creation, Growth, and Development*. Routledge.

Price, Kenneth M., and Ray Siemens, eds. 2013. *Literary Studies in the Digital Age: An Evolving Anthology*. New York: Modern Language Association. https://doi.org/10.1632/lsda.2013.0

Schreibman, Susan, Ray Siemens, and John Unsworth, eds. 2016. *A New Companion to Digital Humanities*. West Sussex: John Wiley & Sons.

Schwan, Anne, and Tara Thomson, eds. 2022. *The Palgrave Handbook of Digital and Public Humanities*. Cham: Springer International Publishing. https://doi.org/10.1007/978-3-031-11886-9

NOTES

1 The *bricoleur* also features in Annette Vee's work on code and writing, and indeed, Vee cites Sherry Turkle and Seymour Papert who, in 1990, argued for the adoption of bricolage in computer science education (Vee 2017, 16).

2 Derrida deconstructs Lévi-Strauss' concept of the "all-knowing" engineer, that no person can be "the absolute origin of his own discourse" (Derrida 1978, 285).

3 I have used these notions of "perverse engineering" and "found technologies" elsewhere in my writing, most notably in my work on how authors are creating born-digital electronic literature (O'Sullivan 2019, 53–54).

4 Those convinced of such an approach to defining DH should engage with the "Doing DH" volumes compiled by Constance Crompton, Richard J. Lane, and Ray Siemens (2016; 2020).

5 This may be doing a disservice to the public humanities, and so readers are encouraged to engage with more thorough treatments of the matter (Jay 2010; Bate 2011; Draxler and Spratt 2019).

6 See the Torn Apart / Separados project:
https://xpmethod.columbia.edu/torn-apart/volume/1/ (Volume I)
https://xpmethod.columbia.edu/torn-apart/volume/2/ (Volume II)

REFERENCES

Bate, Jonathan, ed. 2011. *The Public Value of the Humanities*. Bloomsbury Academic.

Blanke, Tobias, Elena Pierazzo, and Peter A. Stokes. 2014. "Digital Publishing Seen from the Digital Humanities." *Logos* 25 (2): 16–27.

Boyles, Christina, Anne Cong-Huyen, Carrie Johnston, Jim McGrath, and Amanda Phillips. 2018. "Precarious Labor and the Digital Humanities." *American Quarterly* 70 (3): 693–700. doi:10.1353/aq.2018.0054

Crompton, Constance, Richard J. Lane, and Ray Siemens, eds. 2016. *Doing Digital Humanities: Practice, Training, Research*. Routledge.

Crompton, Constance, Richard J. Lane, and Ray Siemens, eds. 2020. *Doing More Digital Humanities: Open Approaches to Creation, Growth, and Development*. Routledge.

Crosby, Alfred W. 1997. *The Measure of Reality: Quantification and Western Society, 1250–1600*. Cambridge University Press.

Derrida, Jacques. 1978. "Structure, Sign, and Play in the Discourse of the Human Sciences." In *Writing and Difference*, translated by Alan Bass, 278–294. University of Chicago Press.

Draxler, Bridget, and Danielle Spratt. 2019. *Engaging the Age of Jane Austen: Public Humanities in Practice*. University of Iowa Press.

Drucker, Johanna. 2012. "Humanistic Theory and Digital Scholarship." In *Debates in the Digital Humanities*, edited by Matthew K. Gold. University of Minnesota Press. https://dhdebates.gc.cuny.edu/read/untitled-88c11800-9446-469b-3be-3fdb36bfbd1e/section/0b495250-97af-4046-91ff-98b6ea9f83c0

Grigar, Dene, and Stuart Moulthrop. 2015. *Pathfinders: Documenting the Experience of Early Digital Literature*. Vancouver, WA: Nouspace Publications. http://scalar.usc.edu/works/pathfinders/index

Jay, Gregory. 2010. "The Engaged Humanities: Principles and Practices of Public Scholarship and Teaching." Imagining America. Syracuse University. https://surface.syr.edu/ia/15

Jockers, Matthew L. 2013. *Macroanalysis: Digital Methods & Literary History*. University of Illinois Press.

Jones, Steven E. 2015. "New Media and Modeling: Games and the Digital Humanities." In *A New Companion to Digital Humanities*, edited by Susan Schreibman, Ray Siemens, and John Unsworth. John Wiley & Sons. https://onlinelibrary.wiley.com/doi/abs/10.1002/9781118680605.ch6

Kirschenbaum, Matthew. 2014. "What Is 'Digital Humanities,' and Why Are They Saying Such Terrible Things about It?" *Differences* 25 (1): 46–63.

Kucsma, Jason, Kevin Reiss, and Angela Sidman. 2010. "Using Omeka to Build Digital Collections: The METRO Case Study." *D-Lib Magazine* 16 (3/4).

Lévi-Strauss, Claude. 1966. *The Savage Mind*. University of Chicago Press.

Liu, Alan. 1996. "Globalizing the Humanities: 'Voice of the Shuttle: Web Page for Humanities Research'." *Humanities Collections* 1 (1): 41–56. doi:10.1300/J139v01n01_04

Liu, Alan. 2012. "Where Is Cultural Criticism in the Digital Humanities?" In *Debates in the Digital Humanities*, edited by Matthew K. Gold. University of Minnesota Press. https://dhdebates.gc.cuny.edu/read/untitled-88c11800-9446-469b-3be-3fdb36bfbd1e/section/896742e7-5218-42c5-89b0-0c3c75682a2f

Mandell, Laura C. 2016. "Gendering Digital Literary History: What Counts for Digital Humanities." In *A New Companion to Digital Humanities*, edited by Susan Schreibman, Ray Siemens, and John Unsworth, 511–523. Oxford: Wiley Blackwell.

Marshall, Kelli. 2015. "How to Curate Your Digital Identity as an Academic." *The Chronicle of Higher Education*. www.chronicle.com/article/how-to-curate-your-digital-identity-as-an-academic/

McCarty, Willard. 2005. *Humanities Computing*. Palgrave Macmillan.

Morrison, Aimée. 2008. "Blogs and Blogging: Text and Practice." In *A Companion to Digital Literary Studies*, edited by Susan Schreibman and Ray Siemens. Oxford: Blackwell. https://companions.digitalhumanities.org/DLS/?chapter=content/9781405148641_chapter_20.html

O'Sullivan, James. 2017. "Computing Differences in Language between Male and Female Authors." *RTÉ Brainstorm*, October 18. www.rte.ie/eile/brainstorm/2017/1018/913307-computing-differences-in-language-between-male-and-female-authors/

O'Sullivan, James. 2019. *Towards a Digital Poetics: Electronic Literature & Literary Games*. Palgrave Macmillan.

O'Sullivan, James, Christopher P. Long, and Mark Mattson. 2016. "Dissemination as Cultivation: Scholarly Communications in a Digital Age." In *Doing Digital Humanities: Practice, Training, Research*, edited by Constance Crompton, Richard J. Lane, and Ray Siemens, 384–397. New York: Routledge.

Piper, Andrew, and Richard Jean So. 2016. "Women Write About Family, Men Write About War." *The New Republic*. https://newrepublic.com/article/132531/women-write-family-men-write-war

Ramsay, Stephen. 2013a. "On Building." In *Defining Digital Humanities*, edited by Melissa Terras, Julianne Nyhan, and Edward Vanhoutte, 243–245. Ashgate.

Ramsay, Stephen. 2013b. "Who's In and Who's Out." In *Defining Digital Humanities*, edited by Melissa Terras, Julianne Nyhan, and Edward Vanhoutte, 239–241. Ashgate.

Rath, Linda. 2016. "Omeka.Net as a Librarian-Led Digital Humanities Meeting Place." *New Library World* 117 (3/4): 158–172. doi:10.1108/NLW-09-2015-0070

Rettberg, Scott. 2016. "Electronic Literature as Digital Humanities." In *A New Companion to Digital Humanities*, edited by Susan Schreibman, Ray Siemens, and John Unsworth, 127–136. West Sussex: John Wiley & Sons.

Risam, Roopika. 2018. *New Digital Worlds: Postcolonial Digital Humanities in Theory, Praxis, and Pedagogy*. Evanston, IL: Northwestern University Press.

Rockwell, Geoffrey. 2013. "Inclusion in the Digital Humanities." In *Defining Digital Humanities*, edited by Melissa Terras, Julianne Nyhan, and Edward Vanhoutte, 247–253. Ashgate.

Ross, Shawna. 2018. "Toward a Feminist Modernist Digital Humanities." *Feminist Modernist Studies* 1 (3): 211–229. doi:10.1080/24692921.2018.1505821

Ross, Shawna, and Andrew Pilsch, eds. 2019. *Humans at Work in the Digital Age: Forms of Digital Textual Labor*. Routledge.

Sample, Mark. 2013. "The Digital Humanities Is Not about Building, It's about Sharing." In *Defining Digital Humanities: A Reader*, edited by Melissa Terras, Julianne Nyhan, and Edward Vanhoutte, 255–257. Ashgate.

Terras, Melissa. 2012. "The Impact of Social Media on the Dissemination of Research: Results of an Experiment." *Journal of Digital Humanities* 1 (3). http://journalofdigitalhumanities.org/1-3/the-impact-of-social-media-on-the-dissemination-of-research-by-melissa-terras/

Underwood, Ted. 2018. "Why an Age of Machine Learning Needs the Humanities." *Public Books* (blog). 2018. www.publicbooks.org/why-an-age-of-machine-learning-needs-the-humanities/

Vee, Annette. 2017. *Coding Literacy: How Computer Programming Is Changing Writing.* The MIT Press.

Weidman, Sean G., and James O'Sullivan. 2018. "The Limits of Distinctive Words: Re-Evaluating Literature's Gender Marker Debate." *Digital Scholarship in the Humanities* 33 (2): 374–390. doi:10.1093/llc/fqx017

Weingart, Scott B., and Nickoal Eichmann-Kalwara. 2017. "What's Under the Big Tent?: A Study of ADHO Conference Abstracts." Edited by James O'Sullivan. *Digital Studies/Le champ numérique* 7 (1). doi:10.16995/dscn.284

3

COMPUTATION FOR CRITICISM

The *Star Wars* franchise has furnished us with many iconic cinematic moments, but few scenes stand as prominently in the popular imagination as that which sees Luke Skywalker skimming the Death Star trenches in his x-wing, the fate of the Rebellion base on Yavin IV resting on his ability to hit a small thermal exhaust port only about two metres wide. As Skywalker prepares to discharge the proton torpedoes intended to destroy the station, he chooses, much to the surprise of his command team, *not* to use his targeting computer. He relies instead on his command of the Force, the mystical, omniscient energy field which binds the galaxy together. This scene is a useful analogy for the current state of play in the arts and humanities, where there is an ongoing struggle between ways of reading which are perceived to be fundamentally different. A growing chorus of scholars wants to move beyond the hokey religions of the past, while others believe in keeping to long-established critical traditions, far more powerful than any technological terror that might be constructed. James Somers, writing in *The Atlantic*, notes how Skywalker's decision to "trust an intuition born deep in nature and honed over billions of lifetimes instead of some

DOI: 10.4324/9781351203395-3

newfangled tech seems somehow right and good," but he probably should have used the targeting computer (Somers 2017). "It's computers," Somers notes, "that help us perceive beyond our senses."

It is odd to see conflicts between "traditional" and "computer-assisted" ways of reading persist. It should be abundantly clear by now that we will need computers if we are to save ourselves, just as we will need human intuition. The reality is that no digital tool or method can be of much utility without other—one might say older—methods of interpretation, and many of the digital humanities' advocates can sometimes be overzealous in their representation of the field's potential to transform existing disciplinary cultures and practices. But there are many questions which human perspective simply cannot tackle alone. As Joseph Weizenbaum, one of the pioneers of artificial intelligence, famously wrote: "Instrumental reason can make decisions, but there is all the difference between deciding and choosing" (Weizenbaum 1977, 259). Using instrumental decisions to answer the complex questions of culture requires a lot of negotiation between human and computer reason, between decisions (calculation) and choices (interpretation), and it is in such negotiations that we see how good DH really operates, at the juncture between the instrumental and the human. Being an acolyte of the digital humanities is not about trusting blindly in computers, it is about knowing your x-wing has one and that sometimes you might use it, sometimes you might choose otherwise. The main thing is that you accomplish your objective, be that blowing up a Death Star or analysing some aspect of culture.

Computer-assisted analytical techniques have allowed scholars from a whole range of disciplines within the humanities to ask new questions and re-engage with old arguments with *different* kinds of statistical evidence. Nowhere has this been more prevalent than in textual disciplines, where computer-assisted techniques are becoming increasingly popular forms of inquiry. Most scholars refer to this kind of computation for criticism as "distant reading."[1] But whatever one calls this practice—"distant reading," "cultural analytics," "computer-assisted text analysis," "computational literary studies," "cultural analytics"—the purpose in doing this kind of work is clear: "Quantitative approaches to literature represent elements or characteristics of literary texts numerically, applying the powerful, accurate, and widely accepted methods of mathematics to measurement, classification, and analysis" (Hoover 2013).

It should be noted that computer-assisted analysis is not solely confined to text: and there is some very innovative and intriguing work being done in areas like "distant viewing" and "visualising voice" (Arnold and Tilton 2019; Ardrey 2020). Still, as far as computer analysis is concerned, text currently enjoys something of a privileged position in the digital humanities.[2] Scott B. Weingart and Nickoal Eichmann-Kalwara show that, while a range of disciplines and practices sit under the DH umbrella, literary studies and text analysis are among the most prominent (Weingart and Eichmann-Kalwara 2017). Indeed, the computer-assisted analysis of text has been central to the digital humanities right from the very beginning, when Busa used his punched cards to automate the production of concordances. As DH has developed, so too has the centrality of text been reaffirmed, and many of the digital humanities' most established tools and methods, as well as the recognisable figures and publications, have emerged from the text-based disciplines and practices. Ascendancy of any sort can suffocate diversity, and one could justifiably argue that a large part of the field's preoccupation with text has acted as an impediment to realising the potential of now unknown technologies and techniques. But text does deserve at least a measure of the privilege it currently enjoys in DH, privilege which has really just been transferred from the wider humanities—text is *essential* to our understanding of society and culture. And with the emergence of large language models, the centrality of text has only increased.

And from a more practical perspective, text is malleable. Unlike, say, visual artefacts, text is particularly susceptible to data-driven analytical techniques, and so we can learn much about text-based cultural materials by breaking them down into their constituent parts and counting those parts. Computers are remarkably good at counting, and while counting seems to be a trivial task, done at scale it can tell us a considerable amount about many things. Comparative to most other forms of expression, text is by far the form upon which we can do the most analysis with the least amount of computing power.

DISTANT READING

Computers are useful in the study of written texts for one simple reason: they allow us to see patterns and trends undetectable through human discernment alone. There is a lot that computers cannot tell us; indeed, the limitations of computer-assisted analysis far outweigh the possibilities, and the results are worthless if turned into poor interpretation by misreading. But properly implemented and understood, the results of a computational analysis can tell the reader much about text-based materials. A similar disclaimer was offered by the late John Burrows in 2002:

> The close reader sees things in a text—single moments and large amorphous movements—to which computer programs give no easy access. The computer, on the other hand, reveals hidden patterns and enables us to marshal hosts of instances too numerous for our unassisted powers.
>
> (Burrows 2002b, 696)

And that, quite simply, is what distant reading is: the use of statistical methods and computer programmes to assist in the revelation of hidden patterns.

From a technical perspective, distant reading includes a very broad spectrum of methods. An example of a basic application of distant reading would be the creation of a most frequent wordlist, so that a reader can see, with a very quick glance, which terms dominate the content of a document. A bit more complicated than a wordlist would be something like collocation or co-occurrence analysis, which groups words based on how often they tend to be used together. Finally, at the complicated end of the technical spectrum are advanced forms of natural language processing and machine learning techniques. Distant reading is a vast domain spanning a great many theories and techniques across statistics, corpus and computational linguistics, natural language processing, machine learning and artificial intelligence.

Distant reading is best understood through a comparison with close reading. Close reading is how we, as individuals, typically consume textual content, scrutinising each word to unpack the layers of meaning. Close reading is quite granular, it allows readers to interpret the nuances in a text, the subtle shades of meaning or expression that are not always obvious unless a lot of attention is given to the ways in which an author has composed a sentence. Distant reading achieves the opposite, it detects the higher order trends and patterns that persist across a broader body of writing. If a reader wants to understand how James Joyce portrays Ireland, then they would be well advised to sit down and read Joyce's novels (and then read them again, and again). This is close reading, and it is an extremely valuable way of understanding documentary materials like literature. But if someone wants to understand how Ireland is portrayed across a broader canon, well then, eventually, close reading just will not do. Given enough time and resources, a diligent and expert reader can intuit an awful lot from a large corpus, but if one really wants to examine text at scale—if they want to examine, theoretically, as many books as have been published—well, the limits of human capacity will soon get in their way.

Distant reading is suited to analyses where the nuances of meaning and expression usually sought through close reading can be sacrificed in the name of some "bigger picture," typically a literary device or element like style and theme. Distant reading might be said to be aligned with formalism, focusing on the structural features, forms, and genres of a corpus, while its emphasis on evidence, often quantitative evidence produced from experiments, certainly makes it empiricist.

Describing close and distant reading as "opposite" is purely illustrative. In practice, the interpretation of data-driven findings will be of little use without a refined appreciation of the materials being analysed, just as readings based on smaller canons and corpora can be limited in scope. Critics reading graphs produced using statistics are just as prone to misinterpretation and generalisation as those who are close reading. As Andrew Piper argues in *Can We Be Wrong?*, a mixed method approach combining machine learning with individual observations seems like a reasonable way to approach textual evidence (Piper 2020). This is not to say it is the only way or the better way, but a *reasonable* way.

Likening the reading practices described thus far in this chapter to the study of economics, Matthew Jockers terms this negotiation between close and distant reading "macroanalysis." Regarding "distance" in reading, he writes:

> Human interpretation of the "data," whether it be mined at the macro or micro scale, remains essential. Although the methods of inquiry, of evidence gathering, are different, they are not antithetical, and they share the same ultimate goal of informing our understanding of the literary record, be it writ large or small.
>
> (Jockers 2013, 26)

By assuming this middle ground, critics can understand the broader systems which persist across corpora and canons as well as have some sense of individual texts which comprise such. It is for this very reason that the term "computer-assisted" is favoured throughout this book: computers cannot replace the critic, but they can help them perceive what might otherwise go unseen.

There is no reading that is entirely distant, because it would be impossible to commit any serious act of interpretation without some measure of context. Unless a reader understands the dataset being analysed, they will be in no position to extrapolate the significance of possible trends, consistencies, anomalies, and outliers. Lines and dots on a chart are just that unless the reader has some deeper appreciation of the data being represented. As Martin Eve puts it: "Using software as a tool to explore texts can lead us to new literary insight, if we retain a vibrant critical, theoretical, historical, and interpretative imagination" (Eve 2020). Equally, that interpretive imagination has much to gain from the processing power of machines, or at the very least, of thinking about language and culture in a more expansive, interdisciplinary manner. In his genealogy of distant reading, Ted Underwood describes how Janice Radway operated at the "boundary between literary history and social science," using quantitative methods in her 1984 text, *Reading the Romance*, to challenge dominant critical views of popular literature (Underwood 2017). Computers, the digital humanities, natural language processing, and machine learning are all just the next step in this lineage. Rejecting the interdisciplinary turn in cultural criticism is a little belated, and worse, betrays some vanity and outmoded faith in individual genius.

Distant reading is not just applicable to vast quantities of text. In his book, *Close Reading with Computers* (2019), Eve demonstrates the value of using computer-assisted methods to explore just one novel, David Mitchell's *Cloud Atlas*. In fact, there are many published examples of distant reading where the emphasis is on either a single or only a handful of texts (Clement 2008; Reeve 2016; Hoover 2017; O'Sullivan et al. 2018; Jarvis 2019). Distant reading is not about the size of the dataset, but rather, the thing that is being sought: as noted, is it a matter of nuance, or a matter of structure and form? The minute or the overarching? Distant reading is a different, quantitative way of reading that can be just as readily applied to individual texts if the purpose is to use macroanalysis to help find latent patterns that might otherwise have been missed. While a computer scientist might balk at the idea that four novels constitute "big data," such is the number of novels written by James Joyce. It would take a very brave scholar indeed to argue that Joyce's oeuvre is not "big" or "complex" enough to warrant computer-assisted consideration. There has been some talk about distinguishing between "big" and "small" data humanities (Kaplan 2015), but the size of the data should be relative to the research question being posed. Whether something can be described as either "big" or "small" serves very little critical function. A well-formed critical question should sufficiently dictate the size of the dataset necessary.

But whatever the size of a corpus, distant reading usually boils down to one thing: *counting*. Distant reading takes novels, poems, newspaper or magazine articles, letters, webpages, film dialogue, tweets, bathroom graffiti, and breaks these texts down into their constituent elements before counting those elements in the hope of learning something about the general ways in which they are written. Many remain horrified by this practice.

Stanley Fish, to cite a particularly famous example, once wrote in *The New York Times* that the problem with the digital humanities is that "you don't know what you're looking for or why you're looking for it" (Fish 2012). Stephen Marche goes further, rejecting the very notion that literature might be thought of as data: "Literature cannot meaningfully be treated as data. The problem is essential rather than superficial: literature is not data. Literature is the opposite of data" (Marche 2012).

There are times when—as one would assume Stanley Fish is aware—serendipity lends you an unforeseen discovery worth pursuing, but for the most part, a researcher would be incredibly fortuitous to build a career out of critical techniques applied blindly. Conducting a computer-assisted analysis of any corpus requires a well-honed research question and methodology: you cannot simply grab a few dozen texts, click analyse, and hope for the best. Without a proper agenda, how would a researcher know what corpus to gather? Which of the many computer-assisted tools and methods would they apply? How would they interpret the results? The reality of distant reading is quite the opposite of what Fish suggests: you really do need to have a very clear sense of what you are looking for before you begin to gather your corpus and implement your chosen method. Despite claims to the contrary, computers are not all-knowing wizard boxes at which you can just throw texts and expect results in return. Computers need to be told what to do, every step of the way, so if you do not know what you are doing or where you expect to end up, it is really quite impossible to end up anywhere. True, there will be the odd scholar who does proceed in this way, unsure of why they are implementing specific steps in a computer-assisted analysis. And as for his "b's and p's" example, that is a nice illustration of what close reading can do that distant reading cannot, but we already knew this; there are things that only close reading will discover, and there are times when distant reading is more appropriate. And most of the time the reality is that DH methods require close and distant reading to be used in tandem.

Marche's critique is a little more substantive, because there is something disconcerting about the ways in which DH methods reduce literature down to cold, unfeeling numbers. But that sentiment has very little to do with critical practice, which has always been a little instrumental: whether close or distant, critical reading involves applying some technique to certain specificities of a text for particular purposes. Critical reading is different from reading for pleasure, in that it is a deliberate, active attempt to analyse and evaluate. Critical reading is always cold, because while one might take much pleasure in its pursuit, it is not a leisure activity, it is a professional practice, and as with any profession, one should use the tools best suited to the task. In certain instances, computer-assisted techniques are just part of a toolkit that the professional literary critic can use. There is no doubting that close reading *feels* more respectful to those acts of literature we all cherish, but whether it is a human or a computer that is parsing sentences and noting words and the patterns they form, in both instances the literature is being treated as data.[3]

In many cases, the thing being sought by a critical reader will be beyond the abilities of distant reading, like complex allusions, or any of those deep, hidden, contextual nuances that elude readers for decades, and once found, divide opinion for many decades more. As Marche puts it, "Literature is irredeemably broken and messy. Its brokenness and its messiness are part of its humanness." And computers are not good at dealing with that which is broken (they are okay with messiness).

But, sometimes, computers can be hugely beneficial to the understanding of a text, particularly if, as already noted, part of the critical approach being taken involves counting. This is where distant reading demonstrates its usefulness; whatever the perceived size, messiness[4] or richness of a text, if counting something simple like word frequency, distant reading can do more than any person. Nobody is saying that literature is data, but if answering a research question can be assisted by counting some element of a text, a computer can help. That may seem offensive to people dedicated to literary appreciation, but it is intellectually blinkered to deny the application of new, or experimental critical techniques to textual corpora simply because doing so does not *feel* right. We owe it to the works of art we all love to continue to further our understanding, however possible, of what it is they have to say about the human condition.

Distant reading detects trends that *are* there, and we should be careful not to confuse the inability of (human) critics to develop valuable interpretations from meaningful patterns, or equally, mistake unremarkable trends for something groundbreaking. Computers work well when used properly: "The computer is merely a tool. It can do some things very well, but much should be left to the judgement of the scholar, both to situate the project in the broader range of scholarship on the particular topic and to interpret the results within the context of other research" (Hockey 2000, 66). Attacking the very premise of computer-assisted techniques as methodologically legitimate because they are not always applied with rigour betrays a desire on the part of some to cling to a status quo ante; it suggests a fear of the not knowing in a profession where knowing is everything. Perhaps there is some socio-economic merit to this fear, as discussed in Chapter 6, but no reader should be afraid of a new tool which can, in the right circumstances, tell us something about the cultural artefacts we value.

MAJOR TOOLS AND METHODS

Novelist and academic AL Kennedy describes cultural analytics of the sort described in this chapter like "hitting a painting with a fish" (Lea 2016). "Why would you?," she asks. There may well be something to be learned from hitting a painting with a fish, but her analogy is a poor one, in that there are many reasons—at the very least, seven (Underwood 2015)—why one would use computer-assisted analysis to understand text. Commentators such as Kennedy need to desist from making unnecessarily aggressive generic arguments of the following kind: "This seems to be a tool that has no purpose, designed by people who don't understand something, on behalf of some other people whose lack of understanding is different but equally profound" (Lea 2016). Not everyone in DH is a hapless victim of the techno craze, stumbling blindly about in a box of algorithms in the hope that they might find an appropriate analytical tool. The arts and humanities, old and new,[5] would be much better served if figures like Kennedy focused on thorough engagement with the very many robust and meaningful treatments of literature and culture that have been conducted in the name of DH (Fischer-Starcke 2010; Jockers 2013; Bode 2014; Rockwell and Sinclair 2016; Piper 2018; Underwood 2019; Allison 2018). This goes back to the intellectual dishonesty noted earlier: sanctimonious arguments around the nature of literature or the utility of tossing fish about serve no one's purpose, so it is time to focus our energy on specific tools and methods, and how scholars actually apply computers in the service of analysing culture.[6]

Johanna Drucker issues a useful provocation in this regard:

> After several decades of digital work, the question remains whether humanists are actually doing anything different or just extending the activities that have always been their core concerns, enabled by advantages of networked digital technology (easier access to primary materials, speed of comparison, searching, etc.).
>
> (Drucker 2012)

In some respects, nothing really has changed: scholars still look for patterns and anomalies, for presence and absence, using the information they derive from texts to produce meaning. That computers have sometimes made this process more efficient, is not all that exciting. Many of the studies being done in DH tell us things we already know, or that we have certainly expected, because it is difficult to develop a robust research question and quantitative experiment without first having a hypothesis. There is value in using computers to validate what we, as readers, have already intuited, but confirmation alone is not really "doing anything different" in the way that Drucker suggests.

But we are being very unfair to computers here, because efficiency, as the foundation upon which complexity is built, constitutes all the difference. Fr Roberto Busa's most lasting contribution to the digital humanities is that he showed us how using search functions to focus on the location of specific words in even the simplest of machine-assisted procedures, can be revelatory in our understanding of texts. Even deep readings of rich texts can be aided by the unforeseen contexts and trends which the simplest computer programmes might reveal. Listing words, however methodologically mundane, can be a powerful critical instrument. However trivial some of the tools and methods deployed in DH might seem, they allow us to know things that would otherwise remain unknown, to see and consider things differently from the ways in which they have customarily been seen and considered.

There are two kinds of methods in the digital humanities: what we might consider "mature" and "fledgling." The mature methods are those which have been around for a long time, and, aside from the occasional revision or incremental advance, enjoy consensus on how they should be applied. While these techniques are not always mathematically trivial, they tend to be on the lower end of the complexity scale: the simpler the logic, the easier it is for a larger group of scholars to accept and adopt an approach. Examples of mature methods would be basic techniques like frequent word lists,[7] which, while relatively easy and perhaps a little unexciting, can tell us a lot about a particular corpus of data (Steger 2013). We might also include techniques like stylometry and network analysis in this category.

Stylometry is a quantitative approach to analysing the linguistic style of texts by measuring various features, such as word frequency, sentence length, and syntactic patterns. It is often used to attribute authorship or to identify stylistic differences across texts. By focusing on the distinct linguistic fingerprints that authors unconsciously leave in their writing, stylometry has become a valuable tool in literary studies, authorship attribution, and forensic linguistics. Network analysis is used to explore the relationships and connections between entities, such as characters in a literary work or concepts within a dataset. It is visualised through nodes (representing the entities) and edges (representing the relationships), allowing for the study of patterns of interaction, influence, and structure. In the context of the humanities, network analysis is often employed to map out social or conceptual networks in data.

While not exactly mathematically trivial, stylometry and network analysis benefit from having been around a long time and have thus developed as robust approaches to computer-assisted analysis and can be applied using readymade tools like Stylo (Eder et al. 2013) and Gephi (Bastian et al. 2009). These methods are mature in the sense that they do not require much of an interpretative leap in terms of application or reception: it is relatively easy to understand how they work, and it is clear in well-established and presented studies what they are telling us about the materials being examined.

"Fledgling" practices are less robust in that they require a little more technical expertise to appreciate the finer points of their application, and scholars in the arts and humanities sometimes struggle to see their critical worth. One might include topic modelling in this category, as it can be difficult for non-mathematicians to appreciate the limiting factors of concepts like latent Dirichlet allocation (LDA), the way in which most topic modelling is done in the digital humanities.

Topic modelling is a computational technique used to identify and explore the underlying themes or topics present within a large corpus of text. Rather than manually categorising or reading through texts, topic modelling algorithms uncover patterns of word co-occurrences that represent distinct topics. Each topic is understood as a collection of words that frequently appear together, and each document in the corpus is represented as a mixture of those topics. This method is particularly useful in exploring unstructured data, such as large collections of documents, and in revealing thematic structures that may not be immediately apparent. Latent Dirichlet Allocation (LDA) is one of the most widely used algorithms for topic modelling. It assumes that documents are composed of multiple topics, and each topic is a distribution over words. LDA works by iteratively estimating the distribution of words across topics and the distribution of topics across documents. The model outputs a set of topics, each defined by a probability distribution over words, and assigns a mixture of these topics to each document, reflecting how much each topic contributes to the document. LDA provides a probabilistic framework that allows researchers to model the hidden thematic structure in large corpora, making it a powerful tool in digital humanities and other fields for understanding textual data at scale.

More "fledgling" still might be word embeddings, a type of representation in which words or phrases from a text are mapped to vectors of real numbers in a high-dimensional space. These vectors capture semantic relationships between words based on their context within a large corpus of text. Unlike traditional methods of representing words that treat each word as an independent entity, word embeddings encode semantic similarities by positioning words that often appear in similar contexts closer together in the vector space. Models such as Word2Vec and GloVe are popular approaches for generating word embeddings. Word2Vec, for instance, creates these embeddings by training on the idea that words appearing in similar contexts will have similar meanings, resulting in vectors that can capture complex relationships such as analogies. For example, the vector for "king" minus "man" plus "woman" produces a vector close to "queen". Word embeddings are particularly useful in natural language processing, as they allow for more nuanced understanding of word meanings and relationships than previous methods.

Digital humanities scholars should not be overly concerned with this distinction between mature and fledgling methods, but it is useful to acknowledge that there are methods in this field which work well and are used often, and there are methods which are still undergoing development. There are methods which have been frequently applied and so benefit from a canon of pre-existing research to which advocates can point, and there are methods which, while statistically sound, have not yet been utilised in many analyses of specific cultural materials. In both instances, there are examples of studies which get things wrong, or which rely on methods that are later improved upon or shown to be flawed.

The fact is that there are several tools and methods within the digital humanities that are used quite widely because many scholars in the field are comfortable with how they work, what they are doing, and what can be determined from the results of any application. And it is in these tools and methods, whether we call them mature, robust, established, that we find the "something different" that Drucker is seeking. Although it is not always fundamentally different in the mind-expanding sort of way, the aid of a computer allows for ways of reading different enough to accomplish feats beyond ordinary human capacity. An example of such a technique, and there are many, is, as aforementioned, stylometry.

Stylometry, or what is sometimes called "computational stylistics," is the ideal technique for illustrating the potential of computer-assisted text analysis, because it is, algorithmically-speaking, relatively easy to understand. It is also a critical approach with a long history that pre-dates digital computing, showing that certain types of criticism benefit considerably from automation. As far back as 1851, long before anyone had even heard of Roberto Busa, British mathematician Augustus de Morgan speculated that measuring the lengths of words throughout the Pauline epistles might settle their contested authorship, a hypothesis which was later tested by Thomas Corwin Mendenhall, an American physicist and meteorologist who used a spectroscope to visually represent and compare word-length distributions across several authors. The speculations of de Morgan and the experiments of Mendenhall initiated what has now become one of the most utilised methods in the digital humanities. Stylometry is all about using style[8] to quantitatively measure how a text is written, typically by counting specific verbal features in a text to form a "signature" or "authorial fingerprint" which can then be used for the purposes of classification. Stylometry is most often used to attribute authorship to disputed texts,[9] such as in the case of the pseudonymous Italian writer Elena Ferrante (Savoy 2017; Eder 2017; Tuzzi and Cortelazzo 2018).[10] Stylometrists have also made original contributions in, among many other subjects, the study of gender (Rybicki 2016; Weidman and O'Sullivan 2018), collaborative authorship (Rybicki 2016; Weidman and O'Sullivan 2018), translation (Burrows et al. 1999; Eder 2011; Rybicki and Heydel 2013; Forsyth and Lam 2014; Waldenfels and Eder 2016), political speeches and controversies (Kubát et al. n.d.; Jockers et al. 2020), creative communities (McCarthy and O'Sullivan 2020; O'Sullivan 2021; Murphy 2024), religious texts (Ledger 1995; Jockers et al. 2008; Sayoud 2012; Elewa 2019), epistolary literature and letter writing (van Dalen-Oskam 2014; Pearl et al. 2017; Nini 2018; Rotari et al. 2020), intra-textual style variation (Hoover 2017), and psychological profiling (Noecker et al. 2013).

"Measuring Joycean Influences on Flann O'Brien" (O'Sullivan et al. 2018) examines the stylistic affinities between two prominent Irish modernists, James Joyce and Brian O'Nolan (who wrote under the pseudonym Flann O'Brien). Stylometry was able to identify where O'Brien, long considered to be a Joycean disciple, most closely replicates his compatriot's style. This is a particularly useful example because it addresses two of distant reading's major misapprehensions: the study shows how computer-assisted analysis can be used to prompt a new investigation of old arguments, and it shows how computer-assisted analysis is usually ineffective unless coupled with close reading. Critics have long explored the relationship between Joyce and O'Brien, but this was the first study to point, with the aid of statistical evidence, to the elements of their writing that are most stylistically similar. Armed with that information, the task then is to attend to the relevant sections using close reading to determine whether what has been discovered is significant, what new insights might be gained from the graphs.

Stylometry, as it is typically practiced, is based on a relatively straightforward premise: people tend to be consistent in the ways in which they write, because any one person will always be working with their own limited command of language. If we count the frequency of all words across a sample of texts, we can very quickly form a statistical impression of how someone writes. The interesting thing about this is that the most frequent words in any text are usually what we might consider to be every day, functions words like "the," "and," "of." The late John F. Burrows, who received the Busa Award in 2001 for his lifetime of achievement in DH, famously began his monograph *Computation into Criticism* with the statement: "It is a truth not generally acknowledged that, in most discussions of works of English fiction, we proceed as if a third, two-fifths, a half of our material were not really *there*" (Burrows 1987, 1). Burrows' point is that as readers we tend to pore over a very select few words when close reading a text, but in doing so, ignore a significant amount of content: nobody has ever remarked on the author's use of the word "the," but it is from the frequency of such words that we can form an accurate statistical profile of how a text is written.

Language is suited to statistical analysis because, as abhorrent as this might sound to those of us who appreciate the aesthetic potential of words, people writing in the same language choose from a finite pool of words and they are bound by a relatively stable set of grammatical rules. The purpose of authorship is to make selections which lead to beautiful expression, but that is really an empty ideological discussion in the context of counting words to identify trends—the reality is that the relative invariance of the elements of language can, in the right circumstances, be easy prey for statistical models. And the common words are not just statistically useful for stylometric tests; their use also makes theoretical sense because "their frequencies should be especially resistant to intentional authorial manipulation, and so should reveal authorial habits that remain relatively constant across a variety of texts" (Hoover 2009, 35). If we are to genuinely engage with stylometry's foundational works (Burrows 2002a; Hoover 2004; Argamon 2008; Evert et al. 2017), then we will find very little statistical or theoretical grounds on which to dismiss the technique as an unsuitable way to approach the analysis of appropriate cultural texts. It is a robust method based on simple, statistical reasoning[11] that has been empirically demonstrated to work,[12] and so resides at the point where a method produces something critically, and empirically significant, while still retaining an intuitive element that allows the professional reader to exercise personal judgement.

Topic modelling is a useful example of a method which is not quite as easy to understand as stylometry, or as foolproof in its application. This is not to say that we cannot find examples of DH scholars who have published critical findings which have relied on topic modelling, but that we must dig a little harder to find topic modelling papers which are not primarily concerned with advances in methodology. The purpose and utility of topic modelling is abundantly clear: "Topic modeling provides a suite of algorithms to discover hidden thematic structure in large collections of texts. The results of topic modeling algorithms can be used to summarize, visualize, explore, and theorize about a corpus" (Blei 2013). Topic modelling is essentially used to produce a macro-level view of words which tend to appear together in a corpus, giving an indication of what Megan Brett describes as "a recurring pattern of co-occurring words" (Brett 2012) that are discussed in a piece of writing: "topic models find the sets of terms that tend to occur together in the texts. They look like 'topics' because terms that frequently occur together tend to be about the same subject" (Blei 2013).

Using a topic model of 1.8 million articles from *The New York Times* (Hoffman et al. 2013), Blei and his collaborators demonstrate how topic modelling can be extremely useful for exploring massive collections of text: "The model gives us a framework in which to explore and analyze the texts, but we did not need to decide on the topics in advance or painstakingly code each document according to them. The model algorithmically finds a way of representing documents that is useful for navigating and understanding the collection" (Blei 2013).

The trouble with topic modelling is that, thanks to user-friendly black-box tools, it can be relatively easy to produce a model of a corpus, but the theoretical underpinnings and the nuances of implementation are relatively difficult to understand compared with other methods being used by DH scholars. In the words of Scott Weingart, topic models are "powerful, widely applicable, easy to use, and difficult to understand—a dangerous combination" (Weingart 2011).[13] It has been some time since Weingart made that assertion, but not a whole lot has changed in the intervening years and topic modelling still presents something of an interpretive vacuum for many scholars in DH lacking advanced technical skills or statistical training. Topic modelling burst onto the DH scene accompanied by a great many intuitive—and still relevant—descriptions of what it does and how it fundamentally works (Weingart 2012; Meeks and Weingart 2012; Underwood 2012). And yet, that did not translate into a plethora of published studies and computer-assisted discoveries, particularly in domains such as literary criticism which have usually been at the forefront of methodological application in the digital humanities.

The inability of topic modelling to better permeate the digital humanities is potentially due to its interpretive obscurity. Researchers and scholars from the natural language processing and machine learning communities have been debating the efficacy of LDA in recent years, and much of this discussion, quite contrary to the progression of areas like stylometry, has taken place without many contributions from the wider DH community.[14] And it is probably not unfair to say that, again, notwithstanding some exceptions, many DH scholars do not entirely understand the subtleties of these debates.

There always seems to be a measure of opacity to studies based on topic modelling. Describing their use of LDA in a topic model of the *PMLA* journal, the purpose of which was to analyse the history of literary scholarship,[15] Goldstone and Underwood note the following: "As you change the number of topics (and other parameters), models provide different pictures of the same underlying collection." This is an example of the bridge that many scholars from the arts and humanities find difficult to cross: if changing fundamental parameters like the number of topics[16] impacts upon the model, how can one have any trust in such findings? Again, many of the discussions surrounding these parameters are framed by jargon that one usually needs specialist training to fully comprehend. The concerns raised by Benjamin Schmidt in his "Dismantling Topic Models in the Humanities," first published in 2012, remain timely: topic models "require major feats of interpretation," though this is something with which most humanities scholars are comfortable, and scholars need to be "extraordinarily cautious" about interpreting the output of certain models (Schmidt 2012).

The level of caution required is also dependent on the corpus being examined. Topic modelling is better suited to analysing corpora that consist of materials that one might consider more "communicative" than "creative." Topic models tend to make far more sense when produced from documents containing well-structured content which focuses on very specific subject matter, such as in newspapers or scholarly journals. When modelling literary writing, the results become a little less effective, and indeed, so open to interpretation that the practitioner will only reimpose their own subjective biases and pre-determined hypotheses upon the material, effectively eliminating many of the justifications for choosing a quantitative methodology.

We can cite Schmidt as a means of summarizing this section: "A poorly supervised machine learning algorithm is like a bad research assistant. It might produce some unexpected constellations that show flickers of deeper truths; but it will also produce tedious, inexplicable, or misleading results" (Schmidt 2012). The same might be said of any method favoured by DH scholars, but topic modelling—and indeed, newer forms of machine learning designed for language modelling and text analytics—can be, to echo Weingart, sufficiently alluring and mathematically complex to be particularly problematic in an interdisciplinary space where not all practitioners are technical experts.

In a domain where the methodological state-of-the-art largely progresses according to advances being made in other, more technical disciplines, the prevailing discourse will always be partially concerned with the latest algorithmic fad. This should not detract from successful applications of computational methods to arts and humanities research, and indeed, there are many areas in which DH practitioners use robust computer-assisted methods to analyse cultural materials and conditions, including, among others, sentiment (Kim and Klinger 2019), network (Graham et al. 2016), spatial (Murrieta-Flores et al. 2016) and temporal analysis (Schwan et al. 2019). Whatever the method in question, the purpose remains consistent: the use of computers to see things that we would otherwise have missed or could not possibly have seen unassisted.

THE FUTURE OF COMPUTATION FOR CRITICISM

Published in 2013 as part of the Modern Language Association's evolving anthology *Literary Studies in the Digital Age*, Julia Flanders, "The Literary, the Humanistic, the Digital: Toward a Research Agenda for Digital Literary Studies" was a milestone for the digital humanities, posing some key questions for the field:

> Can digital literary studies provide a model for how humanists might work at scale without losing sight of why our study matters? To complement this question, here is another: can digital literary studies provide a compelling and distinctive account of interpretation—of how literary scholars might work digitally "close up" in ways that take advantage of the detailed modeling that digital representation affords? How can digital methods help us re-examine the representativeness and the distinctiveness of the individual text in the context of the vast cultural landscape these methods help us grasp?
>
> (Flanders 2013)

In many respects, the answer to Flanders' questions have come in the form of those DH projects and publications which have revealed new things about art, culture, and humanity. But if computer-assisted criticism in the arts and humanities is to have a future, its advocates must turn in greater numbers to the application of distant reading (and viewing) and cultural analytics.

The primary agenda of the digital humanities should not be the development of new methodologies, but rather, the refinement and application of existing techniques to research questions in the arts and humanities. DH scholars should not, however, be entirely removed from pursuing the development of new methods, but if past decades have taught us anything, it is that the techniques we use in this space will advance, to a large degree, with only a little direct input from beyond the technical disciplines. What we really need now is more application of these methods. Scholars working in computer-assisted criticism can respond to Flanders by *doing*, by actually analysing literary, historical, and cultural corpora using computational techniques. It is through the computer-assisted production of novel findings that this field can provide a compelling demonstration of its distinctive value to interpretation and why it should matter to those studying the human condition.

Method and application are not necessarily natural bedfellows, and there is some merit to the argument that the DH scholars should begin privileging the humanities again, letting colleagues from the sciences work out the new methods which can then, once ready, be applied to cultural materials. The danger with that perspective, as has already been suggested, is that there is a strong correlation between the ease with which a method can be applied and its potential to contribute to misinterpretation. Digital humanities scholars who rely solely on other disciplines for methodological advances, may be in danger of intensifying the number of ill-considered or partisan acts of criticism. But putting aside for now any fears of what black boxes might do to literary and cultural criticism, there is something to be said for the claim that we have done enough building for now; it is time to start using what we have built to a far greater degree. The best way to convince others of the value of computers for criticism is to stop the navel-gazing arguments, stop the methodologically grand maths-heavy pronouncements, and start showing results such as *interesting* interpretations that could not otherwise have been produced.

Computer-assisted text analysis has a vital role to play in that process because the digital humanities began with text analysis, and at the present time is, to a considerable extent, about text analysis (Weingart and Eichmann-Kalwara 2017). Matthew Kirschenbaum once quipped on Twitter that the shift towards distant reading has been so strong in the last decade that DH will soon be overtaken by, and rebranded as, "computational literary studies." He was not wrong: there are now dedicated journals and conferences dedicated specifically to computational literary studies.

Suffice to say, there will always be those who, for what can only be described as ideological reasons, will never be convinced. Another Tweet, this time from Ted Underwood, summarises this issue quite succinctly:

> Dear literary critics: when someone shows that they can predict the acceleration of falling bodies, the correct answer is not a) "duh, we already know that they fall" or b) "this is meaningless until you explain exactly how gravity works," or c) "this inquiry is unethical."

We need to live with the perennial naysayers, just as the self-identified critical purists need to live in denial as we advance further into the age of computational language modelling. That is not to say that computer-assisted criticism is not without its flaws, ethical issues, and limitations—but it is here and it is getting exponentially more sophisticated.

Distant reading poses several ethical challenges, most notably, the inability for studies to be reproduced because of vague, opaque, or inaccessible datasets and methodologies. The questions that one can ask with a computer and the answers that will emerge will be significantly impacted by how datasets are constituted. The humanities have always had a reproducibility problem, but that has been exacerbated by the digital humanities, particularly in the area of cultural analytics (O'Sullivan 2019). Critiquing the practice of distant reading, Katherine Bode argues:

> Far from an incidental oversight, the refusal to publish datasets maintains the fiction that literary data are prior to interpretation: it removes the need either to describe the procedures for collecting, cleaning, and curating datasets, or to expose the inevitably selective and limited collections resulting from that construction.
>
> (Bode 2017, 85)

In many instances, copyright restrictions prevent scholars from legally sharing their datasets. Furthermore, the charge of selective and limited collections can be levelled at any form of reading, as there has never been or never will be a complete dataset. Nonetheless, it is difficult to dismiss Bode's suggestion that many studies have failed to sufficiently elucidate their datasets and procedures, and the resultant manipulation or subjective selections. There will always be subjective manipulations and selections, because, as with any act of reading, distant reading is part of the interpretive process. The issue arises, however, when interpretation is effaced, whether intentionally or through oversight. This failing is exacerbated when scholars insist that computer-assisted techniques are objective, claiming the mantle of scientific certainty without really adhering to basic scientific principles.

None of this should invalidate computer-assisted ways of reading, but unless scholars who are reliant on digital techniques are prepared to engage far more transparently with the limitations of their studies, the field will only serve to reiterate familiar subjective biases and tired insights that existed before distant reading promised to free us from fixed canons and personal myopia. This is not just a matter for datasets and corpora; scholars also have a responsibility to "dispel the mysticism embedded" in such tools and techniques so that colleagues without technical training can have a reasonable chance of understanding and thus appreciating all that is involved in distant reading (O'Sullivan 2019). The divide between fields like computational literary studies and literary studies will never be reduced while these two communities continue to act as though the other is either redundant or inane.

However, bridging the digital divide between scholarly communities remains secondary to the task of self-reflection. Distant reading will only have a future if its practitioners recognise that the application of some computer-assisted methods can sometimes be inherently problematic. Consider this in the context of a Zeta analysis, which can be used to show words which are exclusive to one corpus in comparison to another.[17] Zeta will *always* show the difference between two corpora because that is precisely what it is designed to do, and the significance of that difference is entirely dependent on how the research question is framed and how the results are interpreted. Using Zeta in this way works, and it works well,[18] but applying such techniques to a comparison of male and female authors is, for example, considerably problematic (O'Sullivan 2017). Yes, a Zeta analysis will produce word-lists that are quantitatively indicative of how men and women write in comparison to each other, but it leaves unanswered the reason for asking that question in the first place. There may be research contexts in which such a comparison is valid, but using Zeta to examine whether one group is different from another needs to be very carefully handled because such a technique *will* reinforce any difference that is assumed from the outset. Distant reading can bring the rhetorical power of quantitative evidence to the defence of wider cultural studies and conclusions, but it obscures the wider culture if it remains exclusive and formalistic. Scholars in this space should embrace diversity, as it will be a sad day indeed when cultural analytics reaches a point where the role of the inquirer as critic is no longer necessary. The danger arises when practitioners forget that distant reading is still a human craft, that human decisions on how studies are constructed and conducted will influence results. As Hoover reminds us: "Decisions about what to count can be obvious, problematic, or extremely difficult, and poor initial choices can lead to wasted effort and worthless results" (Hoover 2013).

There are limitations to text analytics, and despite all the current attention to new models and techniques emerging out of natural language processing, machine learning, and artificial intelligence, there remains much that machines cannot extract from text, and many techniques that remain unexplainable in the minds of literary and cultural critics. There are, as Nan Z. Da observes, many perceived "technical problems, logical fallacies, and conceptual flaws" (Da 2019, 601) which distant reading and cultural analytics must overcome as we progress towards an increasingly digital future for the arts and humanities.

But it is worth striving towards such a future. While it is now comprised of a great many, and often dissonant, scholarly, and indeed creative, activities, the DH community first emerged out of a fascination with the potential for the computer to be utilised as an instrument for critical inquiry. The very essence of the humanities is criticism, so we need to continually ask the questions of *how* and *why* of ourselves and our machines. Distant reading can show us the unseen, or it can confirm what intuition had already anticipated, but only when implemented in an appropriate and thoughtful manner. It is very difficult to envision a future for criticism that does not involve computation, so it is time that the energy spent advocating either for or against that future is redirected towards actual reading and interpretation, however one wants to go about doing so.

RECOMMENDED READING

Hoover, David L., Jonathan Culpeper, and Kieran O'Halloran. 2014. *Digital Literary Studies: Corpus Approaches to Poetry, Prose, and Drama*. New York: Routledge.

Lemercier, Claire, and Claire Zalc. 2019. *Quantitative Methods in the Humanities: An Introduction*. Translated by Arthur Goldhammer. Illustrated edition. Charlottesville: University of Virginia Press.

Öhman, Emily. 2025. *Introduction to Text Analytics: A Guide for Digital Humanities & Social Sciences*. SAGE Publications Ltd.

Piper, Andrew. 2018. *Enumerations: Data and Literary Study*. University of Chicago Press.

Piper, Andrew. 2020. *Can We Be Wrong? The Problem of Textual Evidence in a Time of Data*. Elements in Digital Literary Studies. Cambridge: Cambridge University Press. https://doi.org/10.1017/9781108922036

Tilton, Lauren, David Mimno, and Jessica Marie Johnson, eds. 2024. *Computational Humanities*. Minneapolis: University of Minnesota Press.

Underwood, Ted. 2019. *Distant Horizons: Digital Evidence and Literary Change*. University of Chicago Press.

NOTES

1 Readers may find Ted Underwood's genealogy of distant reading quite useful (2017); Lauren Klein's "Distant Reading After Moretti" is also recommended (2018).

2 Certainly, it does in this chapter and book, the emphasis being on literature.

3 For a more developed response to Marche, consider Syme and Selisker's "In Defense of Data: Responses to Stephen Marche's "Literature Is Not Data," *Los Angeles Review of Books*, accessed July 6, 2020, https://lareviewofbooks.org/article/in-defense-of-data-responses-to-stephen-marches-literature-is-not-data/

4 This messiness is partly what draws many to the field, particularly scholars with technical expertise interested in overcoming the analytical challenges presented by literature. For more on messiness, see Schöch (2013).

5 A theme central to Amy Earhart, 2015.

6 There are useful surveys of this topic (Stefan et al. 2015; Nguyen et al. 2019).

7 As the foundation of many DH methods, word frequency lists are worth exploring further (Archer 2016).

8 It is worth considering what might be meant by "style" in the context of DH (Herrmann et al. 2015).

9 I have intentionally omitted the many stylometric examinations of Shakespeare and his contemporaries, believing the matter a little exhausted.

10 For examples beyond Ferrante see Uesaka and Murakami (2015), Schöberlein (2017), Iosifyan and Vlasov (2020), and McCarthy and O'Sullivan (2020).

11 The word "reasoning" is fitting because that is all any statistical method achieves: it allows one to make reasoned judgements when faced with both certainty and uncertainty.

12 It is empirical in the sense that, if you run a stylometric experiment with *x* number of different authors, you will typically find that different texts by the same authors always cluster together (as they should). Where a text clusters incorrectly, there is usually some error (such as a problem with the dataset), some obvious explanation (a particular text being an outlier for an author in terms of genre), or you have made a discovery of some sort (and this is where you need to know the texts in question if you are to bridge the gap from discovery to meaning and knowledge).

13 This is in some sense the point that Fish makes: but the issue here is not the tool or its discipline, but rather, a scholar using a methodology they do not fully understand.

14 DH scholars like Ted Underwood, Andrew Goldstone, and Jonathan Goodwin continue to make active contributions to the advancement of the field.

15 It is worth noting that topic modelling is better suited to analysing corpora comprised of materials that one might consider more "communicative" than "creative." Models tend to make far more sense when produced from documents which contain well-structured content focusing on very specific subject matter, such as in scholarly journals. When modelling literary writing, the results become a lot hazier, and indeed, almost too open to interpretation.

16 There is of course work being done on this matter, for example, Sbalchiero and Eder (2020).

17 In other words, Zeta can tell you the words that appear in Corpus A that do not appear in Corpus B, and vice versa. The illustrative example that I use in classrooms is James Joyce versus Virginia Woolf. When compared to Woolf, Joyce favours words relating to Ireland like "Dublin," "Irish," "Catholic" and "God," whereas Woolf, compared to Joyce, uses a lot of gendered terms, like "herself"

and "woman." This is a meaningless but useful example because the results are easy to interpret and they clearly demonstrate the utility of Zeta: Joyce writes about Ireland, Woolf does not write about Ireland, whereas Woolf writes about gender, Joyce does not write about gender.

18 Zeta may be less reliable when used as the basis for authorship attribution tests (Rizvi 2019).

REFERENCES

Allison, Sarah. 2018. *Reductive Reading: A Syntax of Victorian Moralizing.* Johns Hopkins University Press.

Archer, Dawn, ed. 2016. *What's in a Word-List?: Investigating Word Frequency and Keyword Extraction.* Routledge.

Ardrey, Caroline. 2020. "Visualising Voice: Analysing Spoken Recordings of Nineteenth-Century French Poetry." *Digital Scholarship in the Humanities* 35 (4): 737–758. doi:10.1093/llc/fqz073

Argamon, Shlomo. 2008. "Interpreting Burrows's Delta: Geometric and Probabilistic Foundations." *Literary and Linguistic Computing* 23 (2): 131–147. doi:10.1093/llc/fqn003

Arnold, Taylor, and Lauren Tilton. 2019. "Distant Viewing: Analyzing Large Visual Corpora." *Digital Scholarship in the Humanities* 34 (Supplement_1): 13–16. doi:10.1093/llc/fqz013

Bastian, Mathieu, Sebastien Heymann, and Mathieu Jacomy. 2009. "Gephi: An Open Source Software for Exploring and Manipulating Networks." In *Third International AAAI Conference on Weblogs and Social Media.* San José, California. www.aaai.org/ocs/index.php/ICWSM/09/paper/view/154

Blei, David M. 2013. "Topic Modeling and Digital Humanities." *Journal of Digital Humanities* 2 (1). http://journalofdigitalhumanities.org/2-1/topic-modeling-and-digital-humanities-by-david-m-blei/

Bode, Katherine. 2014. *Reading by Numbers: Recalibrating the Literary Field.* Anthem Press.

Bode, Katherine. 2017. "The Equivalence of 'Close' and 'Distant' Reading; or, Toward a New Object for Data-Rich Literary History." *Modern Language Quarterly* 78 (1): 77–106. doi:10.1215/00267929-3699787

Brett, Megan R. 2012. "Topic Modeling: A Basic Introduction." *Journal of Digital Humanities* 2 (1). http://journalofdigitalhumanities.org/2-1/topic-modeling-a-basic-introduction-by-megan-r-brett/

Burrows, J. F. 1987. *Computation into Criticism: Study of Jane Austen's Novels and an Experiment in Method.* Clarendon Press.

Burrows, John. 2002a. "'Delta': A Measure of Stylistic Difference and a Guide to Likely Authorship." *Literary and Linguistic Computing* 17 (3): 267–287.

Burrows, John. 2002b. "The Englishing of Juvenal: Computational Stylistics and Translated Texts." *Style* 36 (4): 677–698.

Burrows, John, Wayne McKenna, and Alexis Antonia. 1999. "Beckett's Trilogy: Computational Stylistics and the Nature of Translation." *Revue Informatique et Statistique Dans Les Sciences Humaines* 35: 151–171.

Clement, Tanya E. 2008. "'A Thing Not Beginning and Not Ending': Using Digital Tools to Distant-Read Gertrude Stein's *The Making of Americans*." *Literary and Linguistic Computing* 23 (3): 361–381. doi:10.1093/llc/fqn020

Da, Nan Z. 2019. "The Computational Case against Computational Literary Studies." *Critical Inquiry* 45 (3): 601–639. doi:10.1086/702594

Dalen-Oskam, Karina van. 2014. "Epistolary Voices. The Case of Elisabeth Wolff and Agatha Deken." *Literary and Linguistic Computing* 29 (3): 443–451. doi:10.1093/llc/fqu023

Drucker, Johanna. 2012. "Humanistic Theory and Digital Scholarship." In *Debates in the Digital Humanities*, edited by Matthew K. Gold. University of Minnesota Press. https://dhdebates.gc.cuny.edu/read/untitled-88c11800-9446-469b-3be-3fdb36bfbd1e/section/0b495250-97af-4046-91ff-98b6ea9f83c0

Earhart, Amy. 2015. *Traces of the Old, Uses of the New: The Emergence of Digital Literary Studies*. University of Michigan Press.

Eder, Maciej. 2011. "Style-Markers in Authorship Attribution: A Cross-Language Study of the Authorial Fingerprint." *Studies in Polish Linguistics*, 6: 99–114.

Eder, Maciej. 2017. "Elena Ferrante: A Virtual Author." In *Drawing Elena Ferrante's Profile*, edited by Arjuna Tuzzi and Michele A. Cortelazzo, 31–45. Padova: Padova University Press. www.research.unipd.it/retrieve/handle/11577/3274069/238296/2018_Tuzzi_Cortelazzo_PUP_Ferrante_9788869381300.pdf#page=32

Eder, Maciej, Mike Kestemont, and Jan Rybicki. 2013. "Stylometry with R: A Suite of Tools." In *Digital Humanities 2013: Conference Abstracts*, 487–489. University of Nebraska–Lincoln.

Elewa, Abdelhamid. 2019. "Authorship Verification of Disputed Hadiths in Sahih Al-Bukhari and Muslim." *Digital Scholarship in the Humanities* 34 (2): 261–276. doi:10.1093/llc/fqy036

Eve, Martin Paul. 2019. *Close Reading with Computers: Textual Scholarship, Computational Formalism, and David Mitchell's* Cloud Atlas. Stanford University Press.

Eve, Martin Paul. 2020. "Distance and Depth." *Stanford University Press Blog* (blog). January 29. https://blog.sup.org/literary-theory/distance-and-depth/

Evert, Stefan, Thomas Proisl, Fotis Jannidis, Isabella Reger, Steffen Pielström, Christof Schöch, and Thorsten Vitt. 2017. "Understanding and Explaining Delta Measures for Authorship Attribution." *Digital Scholarship in the Humanities* 32 (suppl_2): 14–16. doi:10.1093/llc/fqx023

Fischer-Starcke, Bettina. 2010. *Corpus Linguistics in Literary Analysis: Jane Austen and Her Contemporaries*. Continuum.

Fish, Stanley. 2012. "Mind Your P's and B's: The Digital Humanities and Interpretation." *The New York Times*. January 23. https://opinionator.blogs.nytimes.com/2012/01/23/mind-your-ps-and-bs-the-digital-humanities-and-interpretation/

Flanders, Julia. 2013. "The Literary, the Humanistic, the Digital: Toward a Research Agenda for Digital Literary Studies." In *Literary Studies in the Digital Age*, edited by Kenneth M. Price and Ray Siemens. Modern Language Association of America. https://dlsanthology.mla.hcommons.org/the-literary-the-humanistic-the-digital/

Forsyth, Richard S., and Phoenix W. Y. Lam. 2014. "Found in Translation: To What Extent Is Authorial Discriminability Preserved by Translators?" *Literary and Linguistic Computing* 29 (2): 199–217. doi:10.1093/llc/fqt018

Goldstone, Andrew, and Ted Underwood. 2012. "What can topic models of PMLA teach us about the history of literary scholarship?" *The Stone and the Shell* (blog). https://tedunderwood.com/2012/12/14/what-can-topic-models-of-pmla-teach-us-about-the-history-of-literary-scholarship/

Graham, Shawn, Ian Milligan, and Scott Weingart. 2016. "Network Analysis." In *Exploring Big Historical Data: The Historian's Macroscope*, 195–234. Imperial College Press.

Herrmann, J. Berenike, Karina van Dalen-Oskam, and Christof Schöch. 2015. "Revisiting Style, a Key Concept in Literary Studies." *Journal of Literary Theory* 9 (1): 25–52.

Hockey, Susan. 2000. *Electronic Texts in the Humanities: Principles and Practice.* Oxford University Press.

Hoffman, Matthew D., David M. Blei, Chong Wang, and John Paisley. 2013. "Stochastic Variational Inference." *The Journal of Machine Learning Research* 14 (1): 1303–1347.

Hoover, David L. 2004. "Testing Burrows's Delta." *Literary and Linguistic Computing* 19 (4): 453–475.

Hoover, David L. 2009. "Word Frequency, Statistical Stylistics and Authorship Attribution." In *What's in a Word-List? Investigating Word Frequency and Keyword Extraction*, edited by Dawn Archer, 35–51. Ashgate.

Hoover, David L. 2013. "Quantitative Analysis and Literary Studies." In *A Companion to Digital Literary Studies*, edited by Susan Schreibman and Ray Siemens, 517–533. Oxford: Blackwell Publishing.

Hoover, David L. 2017. "The Microanalysis of Style Variation." *Digital Scholarship in the Humanities* 32 (suppl_2): 17–30. doi:10.1093/llc/fqx022

Iosifyan, Marina, and Igor Vlasov. 2020. "And Quiet Flows the Don: The Sholokhov-Kryukov Authorship Debate." *Digital Scholarship in the Humanities* 35 (2): 307–318. doi:10.1093/llc/fqz017

Jarvis, Claire. 2019. "Almost Trollope." In *The Edinburgh Companion to Anthony Trollope*, edited by Frederik Van Dam, David Skilton, and Ortwin de Graef, 13–29. Edinburgh: Edinburgh University Press.

Jockers, Matthew L. 2013. *Macroanalysis: Digital Methods & Literary History.* University of Illinois Press.

Jockers, Matthew L., Fernando Nascimento, and George H. Taylor. 2020. "Judging Style: The Case of Bush versus Gore." *Digital Scholarship in the Humanities* 35 (2): 319–327. doi:10.1093/llc/fqz028

Jockers, Matthew L., Daniela M. Witten, and Craig S. Criddle. 2008. "Reassessing Authorship of the Book of Mormon Using Delta and Nearest Shrunken Centroid Classification." *Literary and Linguistic Computing* 23 (4): 465–491.

Kaplan, Frédéric. 2015. "A Map for Big Data Research in Digital Humanities." *Frontiers in Digital Humanities* 2. doi:10.3389/fdigh.2015.00001

Kim, Evgeny, and Roman Klinger. 2019. "A Survey on Sentiment and Emotion Analysis for Computational Literary Studies." *arXiv*. http://arxiv.org/abs/1808.03137

Klein, Lauren F. 2018. "Distant Reading After Moretti." *Arcade: Literature, the Humanities, & the World* (blog). 2018. https://shc.stanford.edu/arcade/interventions/distant-reading-after-moretti

Kubát, Miroslav, Ján Mačutek, and Radek Čech. n.d. "Communists Spoke Differently: An Analysis of Czechoslovak and Czech Annual Presidential Speeches." *Digital Scholarship in the Humanities*. doi:10.1093/llc/fqz089

Lea, Richard. 2016. "'It's like Hitting a Painting with a Fish': Can Computer Analysis Tell Us Anything New about Literature?" *The Guardian*, 2016, sec. Books. www.theguardian.com/books/2016/sep/15/what-is-the-point-of-cultural-analytics-computers-big-data-literature

Ledger, Gerard. 1995. "An Exploration of Differences in the Pauline Epistles Using Multivariate Statistical Analysis." *Literary and Linguistic Computing* 10 (2): 85–97. doi:10.1093/llc/10.2.85

Marche, Stephen. 2012. "Literature Is Not Data: Against Digital Humanities." *Los Angeles Review of Books*. https://lareviewofbooks.org/article/literature-is-not-data-against-digital-humanities/

McCarthy, Rachel, and James O'Sullivan. 2020. "Who Wrote Wuthering Heights?" *Digital Scholarship in the Humanities*. doi:10.1093/llc/fqaa031

Meeks, Elijah, and Scott B. Weingart. 2012. "The Digital Humanities Contribution to Topic Modeling." *Journal of Digital Humanities* 2 (1). http://journalofdigitalhumanities.org/2-1/dh-contribution-to-topic-modeling/

Murphy, Terence Patrick. 2024. "Is the Individual Idiolect Substantially a Genetic Inheritance? The Case of Edith, Osbert and Sacheverell Sitwell." *Mankind Quarterly* 64 (4). doi:10.46469/mq.2024.64.4.12

Murrieta-Flores, Patricia, Christopher Donaldson, and Ian Gregory. 2016. "GIS and Literary History: Advancing Digital Humanities Research through the Spatial Analysis of Historical Travel Writing and Topographical Literature." *Digital Humanities Quarterly* 11 (1).

Nguyen, Dong, Maria Liakata, Simon DeDeo, Jacob Eisenstein, David Mimno, Rebekah Tromble, and Jane Winters. 2019. "How We Do Things with Words: Analyzing Text as Social and Cultural Data." *arXiv*. http://arxiv.org/abs/1907.01468

Nini, Andrea. 2018. "An Authorship Analysis of the Jack the Ripper Letters." *Digital Scholarship in the Humanities* 33 (3): 621–636. doi:10.1093/llc/fqx065

Noecker, John, Michael Ryan, and Patrick Juola. 2013. "Psychological Profiling through Textual Analysis." *Literary and Linguistic Computing* 28 (3): 382–387. doi:10.1093/llc/fqs070

O'Sullivan, James. 2017. "Computing Differences in Language between Male and Female Authors." *RTÉ Brainstorm*, October 18. www.rte.ie/eile/brainstorm/2017/1018/913307-computing-differences-in-language-between-male-and-female-authors/

O'Sullivan, James. 2019. "The Humanities Have a 'Reproducibility' Problem." *Talking Humanities* (blog). July 9. https://talkinghumanities.blogs.sas.ac.uk/2019/07/09/the-humanities-have-a-reproducibility-problem/

O'Sullivan, James. 2021. "The Sociology of Style: Writing and Influence within Literary Families." *Poetics*. doi:10.1016/j.poetic.2021.101620

O'Sullivan, James, Katarzyna Bazarnik, Maciej Eder, and Jan Rybicki. 2018. "Measuring Joycean Influences on Flann O'Brien." *Digital Studies/Le champ numérique* 8 (1). doi:10.16995/dscn.288

Pearl, Lisa, Kristine Lu, and Anousheh Haghighi. 2017. "The Character in the Letter: Epistolary Attribution in Samuel Richardson's *Clarissa*." *Digital Scholarship in the Humanities* 32 (2): 355–376. doi:10.1093/llc/fqw007

Piper, Andrew. 2018. *Enumerations: Data and Literary Study*. University of Chicago Press.

Piper, Andrew. 2020. *Can We Be Wrong? The Problem of Textual Evidence in a Time of Data*. Cambridge: Cambridge University Press.

Reeve, Jonathan. 2016. "A Macro-Etymological Analysis of James Joyce's *A Portrait of the Artist as a Young Man*." In *Reading Modernism with Machines: Digital Humanities and Modernist Literature*, edited by Shawna Ross and James O'Sullivan, 203–222. Palgrave Macmillan.

Rizvi, Pervez. 2019. "The Interpretation of Zeta Test Results." *Digital Scholarship in the Humanities* 34 (2): 401–418. doi:10.1093/llc/fqy038

Rockwell, Geoffrey, and Stéfan Sinclair. 2016. *Hermeneutica: Computer-Assisted Interpretation in the Humanities*. The MIT Press.

Rotari, Gabriela, Melina Jander, and Jan Rybicki. 2020. "The Grimm Brothers: A Stylometric Network Analysis." *Digital Scholarship in the Humanities*. doi:10.1093/llc/fqz088

Rybicki, Jan. 2016. "Vive La Différence: Tracing the (Authorial) Gender Signal by Multivariate Analysis of Word Frequencies." *Digital Scholarship in the Humanities* 31 (4): 746–761. doi:10.1093/llc/fqv023

Rybicki, Jan, and Magda Heydel. 2013. "The Stylistics and Stylometry of Collaborative Translation: Woolf's *Night and Day* in Polish." *Literary and Linguistic Computing*. doi:10.1093/llc/fqt027

Savoy, Jacques. 2017. "Elena Ferrante Unmasked." In *Drawing Elena Ferrante's Profile*, edited by Arjuna Tuzzi and Michele A. Cortelazzo, 123–139. Padova: Padova University Press. https://www.padovauniversitypress.it/system/files/download-count/attachments/2023-09/9788869381300.pdf

Sayoud, Halim. 2012. "Author Discrimination between the Holy Quran and Prophet's Statements." *Literary and Linguistic Computing* 27 (4): 427–444. doi:10.1093/llc/fqs014

Sbalchiero, Stefano, and Maciej Eder. 2020. "Topic Modeling, Long Texts and the Best Number of Topics. Some Problems and Solutions." *Quality & Quantity* 54 (4): 1095–1108. doi:10.1007/s11135-020-00976-w

Schmidt, Benjamin M. 2012. "Dismantling Topic Models in the Humanities." *Journal of Digital Humanities* 2 (1). http://journalofdigitalhumanities.org/2-1/words-alone-by-benjamin-m-schmidt/

Schöberlein, Stefan. 2017. "Poe or Not Poe? A Stylometric Analysis of Edgar Allan Poe's Disputed Writings." *Digital Scholarship in the Humanities* 32 (3): 643–659. doi:10.1093/llc/fqw019

Schöch, Christof. 2013. "Big? Smart? Clean? Messy? Data in the Humanities." *Journal of Digital Humanities* 2 (3). http://journalofdigitalhumanities.org/2-3/big-smart-clean-messy-data-in-the-humanities/

Schwan, Hannah, Janina Jacke, Rabea Kleymann, Jan-Erik Stange, and Marian Dörk. 2019. "Narrelations—Visualizing Narrative Levels and Their Correlations with Temporal Phenomena." *Digital Humanities Quarterly* 13 (3).

Somers, James. 2017. "Don't Use the Force, Luke—Use the Targeting Computer." *The Atlantic*, 2017. www.theatlantic.com/technology/archive/2017/04/force-computer-vision/522720/

Stefan, Jänicke, Greta Franzini, Muhammad Faisal Cheema, and Scheuermann Gerik. 2015. "On Close and Distant Reading in Digital Humanities: A Survey and Future Challenges." In *Proceedings of the Eurographics Conference on Visualization* (EuroVis). doi:10.2312/eurovisstar.20151113

Steger, Sara. 2013. "Patterns of Sentimentality in Victorian Novels." *Digital Studies/Le champ numérique* 3 (2). doi:10.16995/dscn.235

Syme, Holger S., and Scott Selisker. n.d. "In Defense of Data: Responses to Stephen Marche's 'Literature Is Not Data'." *Los Angeles Review of Books*. https://lareviewofbooks.org/article/in-defense-of-data-responses-to-stephen-marches-literature-is-not-data/

Tuzzi, Arjuna, and Michele A. Cortelazzo. 2018. "What Is Elena Ferrante? A Comparative Analysis of a Secretive Bestselling Italian Writer." *Digital Scholarship in the Humanities* 33 (3): 685–702. doi:10.1093/llc/fqx066

Uesaka, Ayaka, and Masakatsu Murakami. 2015. "Verifying the Authorship of Saikaku Ihara's Work in Early Modern Japanese Literature: A Quantitative Approach." *Literary and Linguistic Computing* 30 (4): 599–607. doi:10.1093/llc/fqu049

Underwood, Ted. 2012. "Topic Modeling Made Just Simple Enough." *The Stone and the Shell* (blog). 2012. https://tedunderwood.com/2012/04/07/topic-modeling-made-just-simple-enough/

Underwood, Ted. 2015. "Seven Ways Humanists Are Using Computers to Understand Text." *The Stone and the Shell* (blog). https://tedunderwood.com/2015/06/04/seven-ways-humanists-are-using-computers-to-understand-text/

Underwood, Ted. 2017. "A Genealogy of Distant Reading." *Digital Humanities Quarterly* 11 (2). www.digitalhumanities.org/dhq/vol/11/2/000317/000317.html

Underwood, Ted. 2019. *Distant Horizons: Digital Evidence and Literary Change*. University of Chicago Press.

Waldenfels, Ruprecht von, and Maciej Eder. 2016. "A Stylometric Approach to the Study of Differences between Standard Variants of Bosnian/Croatian/Serbian, or: Is *The Hobbit* in Serbian More Hobbit or More Serbian?" *Russian Linguistics* 40 (1): 11–31. doi:10.1007/s11185-015-9155-4

Weidman, Sean G., and James O'Sullivan. 2018. "The Limits of Distinctive Words: Re-Evaluating Literature's Gender Marker Debate." *Digital Scholarship in the Humanities* 33 (2): 374–390. doi:10.1093/llc/fqx017

Weingart, Scott B. 2011. "Topic Modeling and Network Analysis." *The Scottbot Irregular*. 2011. https://scottbot.net/topic-modeling-and-network-analysis/

Weingart, Scott B. 2012. "Topic Modeling for Humanists: A Guided Tour." *The Scottbot Irregular.* https://www.scottbot.net/HIAL/index.html@p=221.html

Weingart, Scott B., and Nickoal Eichmann-Kalwara. 2017. "What's Under the Big Tent?: A Study of ADHO Conference Abstracts." *Digital Studies/Le champ numérique* 7 (1). doi:10.16995/dscn.284

Weizenbaum, Joseph. 1977. *Computer Power and Human Reason: From Judgement to Calculation*. W. H. Freeman & Co.

4

DIGITAL LITERATURE

As with Chapter 2, the Modern Language Association's annual convention is a good starting point for the topic at hand. This time we are in Chicago, it is 2014, and delegates are battling the record cold wave brought on by a southerly shift in the North Polar Vortex. In the ballroom of the Sheraton, an exhibition curated by Dene Grigar and Stuart Moulthrop is showcasing "25 years of experimental literary art" featuring artists like Shelley Jackson and Andy Campbell (2014). The Chicago exhibition was the final of three such showings at the MLA, preceded by Seattle in 2012 and Boston in 2013.[1] These exhibitions, hosted as initiatives of the Electronic Literature Organization, are significant in that they represent the moment when digital literature moved from the marginalised to the mainstream of academia. It is not that digital literature was unheard of at that stage, but that it is only in the last decade or so that it has come to be seen as a significant part of the digital humanities; major exhibits at major community gatherings being evidence of such.[2] That digital literature existed on the periphery of DH for so long is quite possibly just a reflection of those tensions between analytics, theory, and cultural studies discussed in Chapter 2, but certainly, it is no

DOI: 10.4324/9781351203395-4

longer as alienated as it might once have been. And it makes sense that digital literature—a domain which incorporates literature, computers, creativity, and criticism—would find a place under the DH tent.

But what do we even mean by "digital literature"? Probably the most oft-cited definition comes from N. Katherine Hayles, who describes a work of digital literature as "a first-generation digital object created on a computer and (usually) meant to be read on a computer" (Hayles 2008, 3). Depending on the author or context, digital literature is variously called "electronic literature," "literary gaming," "small screen fiction," "e-poetry," and, among other labels, "interactive fiction." The popular mantle, certainly in North American contexts, is "electronic literature," as this is favoured by the aforementioned Electronic Literature Organization, an international body of scholars and artists committed to promoting research, pedagogical and creative activity around born-digital literature. Many of the canonical scholarly treatments, coming from ELO-affiliated scholars, favour the term "electronic literature" (Hayles 2008; Rettberg 2019). Consistency in nomenclature is always good, and there is some justification for choosing the word "electronic" over "digital" because the former is a little more all-encompassing in that it includes analogue technologies and old-fashioned, motorised mechanical things. But "digital" has become something of a cultural colloquialism, such that it is now really a convenient word for describing anything to do with computers, screens, or the web (O'Sullivan 2019c, 6). And so this chapter will use "digital literature," not as rejection of any other term, but rather, as a generic catch-all for the myriad appellations one encounters in this field.

Whatever one calls this stuff, Hayles' definition remains valid: digital literature is literature that can really only be experienced on a computer, whatever shape or size that computer might take, including mobile devices, gaming consoles, and so forth. Literature that has simply been displayed on a screen—as is typically the case with e-books and many online journals—does not count because it does not fit the "born-digital" requirement. As explained by Serge Bouchardon, there is a world of difference between digital and *digitised* literature:

> We can retain the idea that the mere fact of being produced on a computer is not enough to characterize digital literature. Digital literature uses the affordances of the computer to dynamically render the story. If an e-reader simply displays text in the way a printed book displays text—the only difference being that to advance the text one scrolls rather than turns a page—this is not "digital literature." It is printed work digitized for optimal display in a portable computational environment. Digital literature is algorithmic. It changes as the reader engages it.
>
> (Bouchardon 2016, 3)

It is useful to think of digital literature as multimodal writing where consequential computation, regardless of whatever else comprises the modal constellation, is an essential part of the make-up. Computation is "consequential" when the presence of the computer or electronic device inherently affects how a piece is experienced by readers. There will always be exceptions to those rules set out by Bouchardon, but generally, if you can print a piece of art or writing and it still operates as its creator intended, it is probably not born-digital. If you can consume a piece of art or writing by simply viewing it on a screen without having to actively interact, it is probably not born-digital. If a piece is only on a computer because that is how someone *chose* to share it, rather than it *had* to be on a computer for it to exist, it is probably not born-digital. Most works that can be considered to be born-digital will satisfy each or most of these conditions. In short, digital literature is that which uses the "complex expressive processes" of digital media (Ensslin 2014, 43) to do something artistic with words. Take the computer away, and the thing is not at all what it was meant to be.

Examples of what might be considered digital literature include hypertext fiction, first made famous in the late eighties and early nineties by the Eastgate School (Maher 2017), as well as other early experiments in net art and writing (Grigar and Moulthrop 2015; Moulthrop and Grigar 2017; O'Sullivan and Grigar 2019), interactive fiction or text adventures (Montfort 2005) like *Zork* or *Façade*; newer videogame-esque titles such as *All the Delicate Duplicates* (O'Sullivan 2017a), walking simulators like The

Chinese Room's *Dear Esther* and *Everybody's Gone to the Rapture* (O'Sullivan 2017b; 2019a), and perhaps even some AAA videogames that privilege or emphasise the hallmarks of literary storytelling. There are many genres of digital literature—augmented reality, Twitter bots, database narratives, recombinant works[3]—such that offering an exhaustive list is not feasible. As Astrid Ensslin explains, the "various degrees of hybridity" demonstrated by differing kinds of digital literature means that this form of expression typically refuses to fall "neatly into generic or typological categories" (Ensslin 2014, 43–44). In the words of Scott Rettberg, digital literature is "a kind of moving target" (Rettberg 2010, 93).

Wherever that target might be in terms of specific ontology right now, what is certain is that digital literature is having its moment (O'Sullivan 2017a). Videogames concerned with more than just play—titles which privilege things like story and language—are becoming immensely popular among the game-playing public. Whether these pieces of art are considered digital literature or videogames or anything else does not really matter, what matters is that authors and artists are starting to realise the aesthetic affordances of interactive media. As illustrated by those titles mentioned in the previous paragraph—each of which achieved considerable acclaim from critics and consumers and were relatively successful as commercial ventures—digital literature is creeping in from the periphery, centring itself as one of the twenty-first century's dominant forms of contemporary expression. Digital literature is no longer the strict reserve of a few pioneers looking to experiment with hypertext. Academic discourse and the cultural conversation remain, for the most part, under the prevailing influence of modes like print literature, film and television, but it is changing, slowly, as more practitioners and consumers look to the digital.

THE HISTORY OF DIGITAL LITERATURE

Historians of digital literature sometimes trace the form's origins to the early fifties, when Christopher Strachey wrote a love letter generating script for the University of Manchester's Ferranti

Mark I computer (Wardrip-Fruin 2008, 163). In 1967, Alison Knowles and James Tenney wrote a digital poem, *The House of Dust*, in FORTRAN, a programming language originally developed in the fifties by IBM, while *Zork*, one of the first well-known works of interactive fiction, was created in 1979 using a DEC PDP-10 computer. Hypertext fiction, as already noted, came to prominence in the early nineties with the rise of the Eastgate School,[4] a generation of authors who used Storyspace, a hypertext authoring system maintained by the publishing house Eastgate Systems, to create hypertext fiction.[5] Of course, this era did not belong entirely to Eastgate and Storyspace, but rather, it was a time during which artists were experimenting with whatever platforms they could get their hands on, including applications like HyperCard and ToolBook (O'Sullivan and Grigar 2019).

Many histories of digital literature reify this lineage: it all began with early experimental works like Strachey's love letters, followed by the first pieces of interactive fiction, and later, the Eastgate School and what now self-identifies as the "e-lit" community, a group of scholars and practitioners governed by the Electronic Literature Organization. There is a slew of reasons why this is a problematic genealogy. There is some disagreement over the extent to which Strachey should be attributed the mantle of the world's first born-digital author, when many might not consider love letters to count as literature, and indeed, the algorithm which produced said letters was possibly more of a technical exercise than an intentionally creative pursuit. It is often unproductive to squabble over what might legitimately be considered the "first" of anything, but the danger in affirming one historical narrative over another is not in false recognition, but in effacing that which should also be recognised. Whether or not Strachey's love letters can be considered among the first works of digital literature is not nearly as consequential as the poignant reality that the world has probably never even known many of the firsts of the form.

There is a great volume of digital literature already lost to us. Early experiments in interactive fiction were conducted at a time when computers were seen solely as specialist scientific instruments. In the sixties, seventies and eighties, most people did not have access to or any familiarity with computers, preventing the pioneers of digital literature from sharing their work beyond very small, closed circles. Even when the Eastgate School emerged and started selling the first works of commercial digital fiction to the wider public, personal computers remained something of a luxury. The history of digital literature is one of "floppies, diskettes, and compact discs" (O'Sullivan and Grigar 2019, 429) many of which saw extremely limited circulation and are now siloed to special collections and media archaeology labs, or worse, entirely absent from the cultural record and entirely beyond any form of historical recovery.

With so many materials being lost or never even known, the history of digital literature is, relative to other literary and artistic forms, incredibly fragmented. Sadly, the case for digital literary history is now being made a little too late (O'Sullivan and Grigar 2019, 431–432). This is partly the fault of the academy, which is only now turning attention to digital literature. Such a lack of regard for the history and preservation of digital literature can be compared to similar issues with cinema:

> future theorists and historians of computer media will be left with not much more than the equivalents of the newspaper reports and film programs from cinema's first decades. They will find that analytical texts from our era recognize the significance of the computer's takeover of culture yet, by and large, contain speculations about the future rather than a record and theory of the present.
>
> (Manovich 2001, 6–7)

Wherever there is a lack of deliberate attempts to document the present, future histories will suffer. Organisations like the Electronic Literature Organization and its associated projects and scholars do important work in alleviating such paucities (Funkhouser 2007a; 2007b; Kac 2007; di Rosario 2011; Walker Rettberg 2012; Emerson 2014; Pawlicka 2014; Rettberg et al. 2015; Grigar and Moulthrop 2015; Moulthrop and Grigar 2017; Heckman and O'Sullivan 2018; O'Sullivan and Grigar 2019; Rettberg 2019) but ELO-centric histories, as with any such association, tend to focus on the theories and practices of their own, inevitably confined community.

A further challenge to the history of digital literature is that it can be difficult, like any cultural history, to separate aesthetic developments from the relationship between things like technology and capitalism, and narratives of progress. When cultural studies did finally come for technology, the field was largely occupied by ideological examinations of new media in the more meta, public and private sphere sense of the term. Even now, there is a lot more scholarly attention given to the effects of the digital on society than there is the intersection between screens and artistic expression. Furthermore, tangential movements right across DIY culture—things like e-zines—suffered from the same dearth of institutional attention, meaning attempts to situate digital literature within broader historical frames are as hampered as analyses confined to aesthetics. The reality is that a lot of this stuff was for just a little too long considered a little too punk, and our understanding of art and literature in the digital age is suffering now because of that.

But not everything has been lost, and while we should always consider the first of anything to be *among* the first, we can say with some certainty that Will Crowther's *Colossal Cave*, often called *Adventure*, is a very early work of digital literature.[6] Thus, it is a useful starting point for this brief primer on digital literature's emergence and development. *Adventure* is, in essence, a choose-your-own-adventure story, wherein players need to explore a cave in search of various treasures (Montfort 2005, 85–93). Such exploration is achieved by entering short commands like "go south" or "yes," with the consequences of a player's action returned by the text prompt:

> You are standing at the end of a road before a small brick building. Around you is a forest. A small stream flows out of the building and down a gully.
> > walk north
> You are in open forest, with a deep valley to one side.

What is particularly useful about the work's setting is that a cave is a useful way of understanding the underlying topological structure by which *Adventure* is modelled,[7] a structure which represents the fundamental difference between print and digital literature. The narrative structure, like a cave, comprises a series of different caverns containing content, each of which is connected via different tunnels or paths. The order in which caverns are explored, the narrative path that is walked, is at the player's own choosing.

We can really think of any work of digital literature—indeed, any hypertext—as a colossal cave, a series of caverns (content) connected by tunnels (links). Caverns are where the meat of the story is to be found, they are where the authors of digital literature hide the material—textual or otherwise—that one needs to piece a story together. In print literature, readers pass through the caverns in a nice linear fashion, such that there is no real sense of exploration, no fear of missing some content on account of a wrong turn. Borrowing from Barthes, many scholars of digital literature refer to such caverns or pockets of content as "lexias." Digital literature then is really just "blocks of text," or lexias, "and the electronic links that join them" (Landow 1992, 4). Navigating the tunnels between these blocks of texts, or how one explores each cavern, is commonly called a "traversal" (Landow 1992, 123).

The sophistication of lexias has advanced considerably in recent years, such that "blocks of text" is not all one encounters in the cavern. Equally, the traversal routes, the "electronic links" between lexias, are now extremely complex. Where a traversal once required a link to be clicked or, as in the case of *Adventure*, a simple command to be typed, readers and players are now faced with rich, immersive spaces to explore in the pursuit of lexia. But however multimodal a lexia, however interactive and seemingly non-linear a route of traversal, the fundamental schematic of the cave remains somewhat present. This can even be said of new, big-budget, open world videogames set in vast virtual worlds. However it might appear otherwise, players are always exploring cavernous structures which have been pre-defined. The lexias to encounter are vast, and the tunnels between them almost beyond count, but mathematically, all digital fictions exist within computationally-defined, confined spaces.

Whatever the contemporary situation, this underlying structure of lexias and links was explicitly apparent in the early days of digital literature, when the choose-your-own-adventure model dominated the form. This persisted into the eighties and nineties with Eastgate titles like Michael Joyce's *afternoon, a story* and Shelley Jackson's *Patchwork Girl*, which are, as Robert Coover put it during his keynote at the Digital Arts and Culture Conference hosted in Atlanta in 1999, the "early classics" (Coover 1999). Coover's speech was titled "Literary Hypertext: The Passing of the Golden Age," appropriate considering that it would be another decade or two before practitioners started to innovate with digital literature to the same degree as Eastgate's pioneers. Always remember that hypertext fiction was at that time a very novel concept.

This is not to say that some print-based authors had not challenged notions of linearity within the confines of their medium, and some of what was achieved might be considered "hypertextual" in a metaphorical sense. But the Eastgate authors were creating a new kind of narrative anatomy, fictions framed by a hypertextual architecture that was as mathematical as it was metaphorical. While one can argue against the idea of narrative freedom in a philosophical sense, these works were the first to make readers and players *feel* like they were making choices, and that sense of agency, however limited, was nothing short of radical. Part of what made this age so golden was the advent of the personal computer. By the late-1970s, Apple IIs, TRS-80 Model Is, and Commodore PETs were increasingly appearing in domestic settings, and people could get lost in the forking paths of *Adventure* at home or ring up Eastgate and order a copy of the latest hypertext fiction to be sent out as a floppy disk.

Unfortunately, that buzz would soon turn to indifference as a period of relative stasis set in. As the century turned, the world of digital literature seemed for a bit to be a little humdrum. It is not that the form was without innovation or the community without talent, but after such a period of upheaval it is only natural that invention would seem to slow. The advent of digital literature coincided with the emergence of the commercial videogame industry, and throughout the early noughties, much of the academy and public focused their attention on the latter. The little excitement that continued to surround digital literature was generated by scholar-practitioners experimenting with found technologies for partly critical reasons (O'Sullivan 2019c, 65), perversely engineering new commercial tools like Shockwave and Flash for literary purposes.

But works of digital literature produced in such platforms generally failed to capture any real popular attention. The first works of interactive fiction turned early experiments in conversation simulation into processes for storytelling, and publishers like Eastgate brought commercial hypertext fiction into the home for the first time. Literary experiments that came after just could not keep pace with the entertainment promised by commercial videogames, and the idea of digital literature soon fell out of public consciousness. Popular audiences played videogames designed to challenge and entertain, while those interested in experimenting with language and computers went their own way and did their own thing. And for at least a while, digital literature was dead.

CONTEMPORARY DIGITAL LITERATURE

Is digital literature just one big anti-climax? Such was the question posed by Andrew Gallix in a 2008 piece published in *The Guardian* (2008). Gallix is partly offering the old "what about *The Garden of Forking Paths*" rebuttal, pointing to digital literature's failure to diverge with any great significance from print literature's long lineage of innovation:

> Generative poetry simply adds a technological twist to Tzara's hat trick, the surrealists' automatic writing or Burroughs' cut-ups. Interactive fiction has its roots in Cervantes and Sterne. Hypertexts seldom improve on gamebooks like the famous Choose Your Own Adventure series, let alone BS Johnson's infamous novel-in-a-box. Besides, if you really want to add sound and pictures to words, why not make a film?
>
> (Gallix 2008)

There are certainly many parallels to be drawn between the hallmarks of digital literature and its print predecessors (di Rosario

2011; Funkhouser 2007b), but one would expect any artistic form to mirror aspects of its antecedents. Nobody is suggesting electronic hypertexts are the first and only hypertexts, and that the choose-your-own-adventure typology did not begin with print. But because these different forms of literature are similar does not mean they are the same and setting the very first experiments in digital literature against the far longer and thus inevitably richer heritage of print innovation is not really a fair comparison.

But it has now been almost two decades since Gallix published his provocation, and it is encouraging to see that the contemporary moment is one in which the potential of digital literature is turning into something more substantive. Titles like *Dear Esther* and *All the Delicate Duplicates* have brought text-based storytelling to rich, vibrant gamespaces, merging the expressive power of language with the immersion of present-day computer graphics. The difference between print and digital literatures is now extremely pronounced. Most notably, the fictitious worlds that readers of contemporary digital literature inhabit can be multimodally rendered by the author.

Of course, for literature to be multimodal it does not need to be digital, but one who cannot see the difference between present-day digital modalities and those of print is possibly not at all familiar with either. And what the digital can do now has remarkably evolved from what could be done when it was first co-opted to the cause of narrative. Contemporary gamespaces greatly enhance the sense of agency and exploration, discovery and denial experienced by the first readers of interactive fiction, replacing command-line descriptions of surrounds with realistic, navigable 3D worlds. Tools that give authors expressive control over the explicit construction of how settings and characters look and feel, while simultaneously lulling readers into a false sense of liberation from narrative structure, are powerful aesthetic instruments. Perhaps the early creators of digital literature envisioned a day when such would be possible, but certainly, they were not widely available in those pioneering days of the seventies and eighties.

But have titles like *Dear Esther* and *All the Delicate Duplicates*—both walking simulators (O'Sullivan 2023)—really rejuvenated digital literature, or are they something else entirely? Gallix's final proposition on the matter of digital literature's demise is that the form is no longer reliant on language for creative expression and is thus no longer *literary*—digital literature is dead because any literature that the form once offered has been suffocated by technology. He cites Mark Amerika, who speaks of "digitally-processed intermedia art," concluding that the future of digital literature is one which will have "less and less to do with literature." The past two decades have witnessed many great achievements in digital storytelling—*The Stanley Parable, This War of Mine, PRY, What Remains of Edith Finch*—but can these works be considered as digital literature? Or is digital literature, some four decades since it first emerged, still just about text-based choose-your-own-adventure stories and academic experiments in generative, algorithmic writing?

If works such as the aforementioned are not digital literature, then what is? If it is just social media bots and Twine stories (Flores 2019), well then digital literature might as well be dead.[8] Arguing over the exact definition of that "institutionless institution" (Derrida 1992, 42) would be both tiresome and beyond the scope of this book, particularly as most readers probably already appreciate the difference between technical writing designed solely to communicate specified information and writing as an act of creative expression. We know literature when we see it, and we have a very good sense of the aesthetic and cultural traditions to which anything classified as literature must subscribe. Central to the literary tradition is language, using words as written text as the primary device for the delivery of narrative. Certainly, there was a time when digital literature satisfied literature's written word criterion; early, command-prompt interactive fictions like *Adventure* were comprised entirely of text. But the present situation is very different, and while we can count *Dear Esther, PRY,* and *This War of Mine* as having artistic merit, they are not primarily text-based works.

To overcome this issue, Hayles suggests a distinction between "literature" and "the literary," arguing that "creative artworks that interrogate the histories, contexts, and productions of literature" are of great importance to the latter (Hayles 2008, 4). For Hayles, the literary has a lot to do with literature—as one might expect—but is also a broader condition of knowledge that seeps into and draws from disciplines like cultural studies, postcolonial studies, and popular culture (Hayles 2008, 5). Hayles is prompting us to think of the literary as the practical means through which we go about interpreting art and expression in a more wholistic sense. Borrowing the term used by geneticists to describe adaptive mutations, Hayles likens contemporary digital literature to a "hopeful monster" informed by computer games, film, animations, digital arts, graphic design, and electronic visual culture (Hayles 2008, 4). Films can be literary without being literature. Videogames can be literary without being literature. Most art forms, digital or otherwise, could be discussed in similar terms, as monsters which have mutated through a myriad of contexts and crafts. Whether studying literature, film, videogames, or fine art, we draw from a shared and interconnected set of critical theories, such that digital literature of the sort we are starting to see created now, regardless of whether or not it counts precisely as literature in the most sacred sense, responds to literary interrogation. This is why interdisciplinary is slowly becoming the natural order of interpretation in the arts and humanities—you cannot separate forms of cultural expression as readily as might once have been the case. And as Hayles contends, sometimes calling something literature is the best way to facilitate such interrogation, as it forces ourselves and others to reflect on the idea of literature and what the form represents (Hayles 2008, 4). The literary has long been seen as a gateway to understanding art and culture, and it should be no different here.

But this is possibly more of a disciplinary than aesthetic argument, and we must return to Gallix and his claim that digital literature is anti-climactic. When we think of literature, we do not just think of text, we think of story, setting, characters and themes. A work of digital literature might be seen as a lot of things, such as a videogame or piece of "intermedia art," before being seen as literature, but the term, in the present moment, typically refers to computer programs which privilege narrative. Increasingly those programs take the shape of immersive, game-like spaces, where play is an important part of the monster, but no more than the story being told. Where *Adventure* once offered "concise prose that calls interesting details to the reader's attention" (Jerz 2007), the world the author envisions is now right there, thanks to cutting-edge graphics, to be *experienced* rather than imagined or seen. And in some instances, the written element of literature has not even been effaced, such as in *Dear Esther*, wherein the story is revealed through a series of monologues that appear as blocks of text as the player traverses the piece's island setting. This text is not more important than the digital world the player inhabits, the things they see and hear as they walk from one point to another, but it is no less important—the weight of importance does not really matter because the monster would be a different creature altogether were the balance of modalities altered in one way or the other.

Compared to *Dear Esther, This War of Mine* is more concerned with play, with presenting objectives that must be overcome should the player "beat" the game, and yet, it is full of literary things, placing major importance on setting and character, it is fiction designed to explore our morality and society in sad, precarious times. Perhaps this does constitute literature, but does that really matter? We do not look at other categories of art and immediately query typology, we seek out those aspects of the aesthetic makeup we deem most curious, and we apply the most valid critical frame in any given context. Returning to Gallix, digital literature is not dead. Works of digital literature which privilege text while also availing of exciting new immersive technologies are rare, but they do exist. Works of digital literature which privilege exciting new immersive technologies and retain elements of the literary are plentiful. The canon of digital literature may be very wide or very narrow depending on what one counts as literary, but when Gallix asks, "when was the last time you curled up in bed with a hypertext?" (Gallix 2008), I think there are many who would answer that they often do just that.

But if digital literature has really emerged from its stasis, what does it now look like? Consider two critically acclaimed works of contemporary digital literature: The Chinese Room's *Dear Esther*, and *PRY*, developed by Tender Claws. Of the two pieces, *Dear Esther* is undoubtedly the most "game-like," in that players navigate a three-dimensional gamespace designed to replicate a

Hebridean island. Written by Dan Pinchbeck, *Dear Esther* looks and feels like a game: you must move your character around a fictional world, working towards a final, game-ending objective. Many of the hallmarks of a videogame are missing—there are no enemies to fight, no objects to collect, no real way to die—and the only real mechanism in the game is walking, and that is what the player does, from one side of the island to the other. While doing so, the story is played out through blocks of verbal texts—or lexias—which are superimposed on the screen, such that the player ends up reading interior monologue very much in the tradition of the novel. It is in these text-based monologues, revealed as the player explores the island, that the story is revealed and its meaning can be analysed. It is clear to see how *Dear Esther*, relying so heavily on text as an aesthetic instrument, might be considered a work of literature. But it is also a videogame, and even if the play amounts to little more than walking through the game world, such a three-dimensional spatio-temporal framework has come to be a defining characteristic of the form. With *Dear Esther*, one can see how the terms "digital literature" and "literary games" are often interchangeable, and how the contemporary moment for this form is one in which play and the literary make for natural bedfellows. Sophisticated computer graphics make the player feel totally immersed in the story world, while text is used to reveal the story that the player—or reader—is there to uncover. *Dear Esther* is not primarily a text-based work, but it needs text to be what it is, almost as much as any work of literature.

PRY provides a fitting example of what digital literature should be in the twenty-first century, particularly as it was produced by a very small studio formed by two independent artists, Samantha Gorman and Danny Cannizzaro. Despite its modest cast of contributors, it stands as the antithesis of the many facile bots and click-a-lot Twine stories that one sometimes encounters in this space. *PRY* achieves a literary quality that is often lacking in computer-based experiments in writing and creative expression. But *PRY*, unlike *Dear Esther*, is not simply a text framed in an immersive, digital world, it is part film, part text, part audio, part visual art, and part interactive fiction. The clear division between text and game found in *Dear Esther*—the player actively traverses a digital, immersive world, but progresses the narrative by reading lexias of text—is far less explicit in *PRY*. The reader/player/viewer might be at any one time watching a fragment of film, using gestures to switch between a character's sight and subconscious, or deciphering a rich audio-visual composition. Sometimes text is privileged, other times it is effaced. It is an inherently multimodal work of storytelling, and while text is there, so is everything else. But *PRY* remains intensely literary, both in trivial ways, like the bookish presentation of its seven episodes as "chapters," and in compelling interpretive ways. This is a work that uses the hallmarks of literature—language, text, story, place, perspective—to explore and challenge social matters and philosophical ideals.

There are digital acts of storytelling from which text is completely absent, both socio-cultural treatments of serious issues, like *This War of Mine*, and more entertainment-centric AAA videogames like *Horizon: Zero Dawn* and *Horizon: Forbidden West*. The case for *This War of Mine*—a character-driven treatment of civilian experiences and morality during times of war—being literary could well be made, but there is a marked distinction between works like *Dear Esther* and *Horizon*. There are certain aspects of the literary contained within the latter—complex characters, moral judgements, swathes of social commentary—but the elements of play are privileged over any such content. The story in the *Horizon* series, however well-written, is really secondary to the mechanics of the game and the things that players can get up to while in that fictional world. *Horizon* was not developed, and certainly, nobody plays it for literary reasons, and to argue otherwise is to wilfully dismiss the difference between a game that is intentionally literary, and a game with a good story.

But certainly, we can see that the idea of digital literature, particularly now in an age where so much creativity and expression is fundamentally screen-based, can be a very inclusive term. Some scholars might disagree and argue that language must remain at the centre of anything that is to be labelled "digital literature," but it seems as though these things exist on something of a continuum of literariness, or what Ensslin calls the "literary-ludic spectrum"

(Ensslin 2014, 38). On one end of the spectrum you have works which really foreground language and text, while on the other, play is privileged. But wherever a work might sit on this continuum, being intentionally literary is a must for anything to be classified as digital literature. Works like *Dear Esther*, *Everybody's Gone to the Rapture*, *PRY*, and *All the Delicate Duplicates* are intentionally literary, and thus represent what digital literature has become in an age of sophisticated, immersive digital technologies and platforms. The creators of these pieces are no more innovative than those who first set about creating interactive and hypertextual fiction back in the seventies, eighties, and nineties, but when one examines *Dear Esther* alongside *Patchwork Girl*, the difference between digital literature in a contemporary context and what came before is abundantly clear. Literature set in immersive, highly interactive, vibrant digital gamespaces is what should be expected of the form in this present moment. Text should be a part of that literature, but it need not necessarily be privileged as was once the case.

THE FUTURE OF DIGITAL LITERATURE

There is something inherently satisfying in the way that digital literature's first definitions remain valid, and that will likely remain the case for a long time to come. Writing back in 1997, Espen J. Aarseth argued that the difference between print and digital literature is that, with the latter, "it is possible to explore, get lost, and discover secret paths … not metaphorically, but through the topological structures of the textual machinery" (Aarseth 1997, 4). That fundamental difference—the difference between exploration and discovery of the metaphorical and mathematically-structured sort—is all the difference. And in the decades since digital literature first emerged, that really has not changed. Even in the immersive, technically complex digital worlds that one encounters in contemporary works of digital literature, there is always an underlying topological structure being determined by the textual machinery. The readerly choice granted by vast, seemingly-alive digital worlds is an illusion—a powerful and hugely significant one—but an illusion nonetheless (O'Sullivan 2017b; 2019b).

No matter the richness of those multimodal layers which envelope the underlying textual machinery, it all comes back to lexias and links, blocks of content and the paths to be traversed in-between. You can think of any cybertext—old or new—as a themepark. Some themeparks are large, open spaces filled with all kinds of sights and sounds, others are smaller and could do with some renovation; the site and finish of the park adds to the experience, but the schematic is always the same, people move from one ride to the next.

Expand this notion into the most dynamic of gamespaces, a AAA title like Rockstar's *Red Dead Redemption 2*: the navigable world seems impossibly vast with endless places to discover, all teeming with characters, life and objects with which the player can interact. Even a major commercial open world videogame can be reduced to the underlying mathematical structures: those open plains, those hills and valleys and the horses you ride through them are all just paths between the various cutscenes and objectives—the lexias—which progress the content. All games, all digital literature, regardless of where a work fits on the continuum of textuality, is structured on the concept of hypertextuality in its simplest form, bits of content linked in a way that gives some agency, but remains a pre-determined structure. As already noted, this does not mean print and digital literature are the same thing, because that belief in agency is aesthetically potent, and the chance to lull readers into a sense of self-determination within a fiction is precisely what the digital affords. But if the underlying mathematical structures are fundamentally the same, what is the future of digital literature?

For one thing, too much credence can be placed in the argument just offered: the philosophical idea of underlying hypertextual structures and the real, technical, reader-facing reality of the state-of-the-art are two very different things. It is possibly a little too "academic" to argue that digital literature is philosophically unchanged when the experience of contemporary work is radically different to all that came before. Lexias and forking aside, where early pioneers of digital literature had to rely on text alone for his storytelling, the new generation of authors working in this space have the potential to produce incredibly immersive environments for their readers. In terms of narrative devices and aesthetic instruments, it is not at all the same thing. And if one considers the enormous advances between early works such as *Adventure* or *Patchwork Girl* alongside the likes of *Dear Esther* and *Everybody's Gone to the Rapture*, it is exciting to speculate as to what might be coming next.

The more real something seems the more immersed you feel. In only a few short decades we have gone from entirely text-based hypertext fiction to three-dimensional fictional digital spaces that look and sound hyper-realistic and can be explored by readers and players enjoying a heightened sense of agency. Whatever comes next—be that virtual and augmented reality, generative AI based works, or some other unknown technology—has the potential to enhance that immersion. And perhaps artificial intelligence and large language models will soon mean that the spaces in which digital stories are told can swap out the illusion of freedom for real, technical freedom.

Where once a horizon was not just a visual prop but also hard edge to a work's explorable terrain, impassable by the player because there is quite simply nothing beyond, because nothing was programmed to be there, a horizon might now become the point where AI generates some new place, some other part of the story into which the reader might venture. Take *No Man's Sky*, a game which removes such hard edges, the barriers to traversal, by procedurally generating new space and places to explore as players venture further into the cosmos (Morin 2016). The hand of an author might yet be required for some time to come, not just from a philosophical perspective, but aesthetically, there is something inherently monotonous and clunky about the places that generative algorithms like players find in *No Man's Sky* produce (O'Sullivan 2024). But more might be achieved in the decades to come.

And while the procedural generation of immersive, visually vibrant gamespaces is technically one thing, the generative production of text is a much lesser feat. As it was with the early creators of interactive fiction, partly inspired by the time's nascent fascination with "chatbots" designed to replicate human interaction, future creators of digital literature may look to AI for procedural storytelling. With mobile games like *AI Dungeon* and new studios such as Hidden Door, which plans to build natural language processing systems for AI-driven storytelling, already exploring such techniques, that future is seemingly not so distant. The role of the author then, perhaps, will be in the crafting of the AI rather than the story, the source code and algorithms from which some inhuman story emerges. It might not make for good literature, indeed, there will be many who will argue it is not even literary, but it will be aesthetically fascinating to see such technologies mature. It would, at the very least make us reconsider, as we should always do, "our assumptions of what literature can do and be" (Hayles 2007).

But whatever digital literature's aesthetic future, it will be interesting to see whether its critical future gravitates closer to the digital humanities, or even literary studies, or whether it will remain the reserve of those working in electronic literature and videogame studies. DH, a field where one encounters those who would appreciate both the underlying computational structures and the metaphorical layers on top, seems like a natural place for the study of digital literature. The digital humanities are full of tinkerers, students and scholars looking to experiment and hack, people positioned to adapt digital tools and platforms to literary purposes. Were digital literature to become more canonical in our lecture theatres and programmes, interdisciplinary or otherwise, one can see how young people, the majority of which tend to embrace all things digital, would be made to reconnect with expressive language and the craft of writing. That is not to say that digital literature can save its print counterpart, but perhaps the future is one in which the two can help each other.

RECOMMENDED READING

Aarseth, Espen J. 1997. *Cybertext: Perspectives on Ergodic Literature*. Baltimore: The Johns Hopkins University Press.

Chasar, Mike. 2020. *Poetry Unbound: Poems and New Media from the Magic Lantern to Instagram*. New York: Columbia University Press.

Ensslin, Astrid. 2014. *Literary Gaming*. Cambridge, Massachusetts: The MIT Press.

Hayles, N. Katherine. 2008. *Electronic Literature: New Horizons for the Literary*. Notre Dame, Indiana: University of Notre Dame Press.

Rettberg, Scott. 2019. *Electronic Literature.* Polity Press.

NOTES

1 Dene Grigar led the initiative and was a consistent presence on each of the curatorial teams. She co-curated the Seattle exhibition with Kathi Inman Berens and Lori Emerson, while in Boston the curation was led by Grigar and Inman Berens. A curatorial statement by Grigar and Inman Berens can be found as follows: https://dtc-wsuv.org/mla-exhibits/mla-exhibits/Welcome.html

2 Readers looking for further discussion of electronic literature and the digital humanities would be well served by Rettberg (2016), Saum-Pascual and Rettberg (2020), and Dene Grigar's introduction to *Electronic Literature as Digital Humanities: Contexts, Forms, and Practices* (Grigar and O'Sullivan 2021).

3 Accounts of many such genres can be located in *Electronic Literature as Digital Humanities: Contexts, Forms and Practices* (Grigar and O'Sullivan 2021).

4 For more on what many scholars consider to be the "first generation" of electronic literature, see *Pathfinders: Documenting the Experience of Early Digital Literature and Traversals: The Use of Preservation for Early Electronic Writing* (Grigar and Moulthrop 2015; Moulthrop and Grigar 2017).

5 It is worth noting that Hayles refers to the Eastgate School as the "Storyspace School" (2008, 6).

6 Montfort discusses a number of projects which pre-date *Adventure* in his book, *Twisty Little Passages* (2005, 81–85).

7 For a detailed analysis of how *Adventure* is structured and its explicit connections to caving, Jerz (2007).

8 I do not mean to appear over-critical of experiments in language that use platforms like Twitter and authoring tools such as Twine. However, I do think the Twitter bot genre, however critically interesting, is extremely limited as a form of literature, while most Twine stories I have seen, a few notable exceptions aside, were lacking in any real innovation and, unfortunately, quite forgettable.

REFERENCES

Aarseth, Espen J. 1997. *Cybertext: Perspectives on Ergodic Literature.* Baltimore: The Johns Hopkins University Press.

Bouchardon, Serge. 2016. "Towards a Tension-Based Definition of Digital Literature." *Journal of Creative Writing Studies* 2 (1). http://scholarworks.rit.edu/jcws/vol2/iss1/6/

Coover, Robert. 1999. "Literary Hypertext: The Passing of the Golden Age." Keynote presented at the Digital Arts and Culture, Atlanta, Georgia, October 29. http://nickm.com/vox/golden_age.html

Derrida, Jacques. 1992. "This Strange Institution Called Literature: An Interview with Jacques Derrida." In *Acts of Literature*, edited by Derek Attridge. London: Routledge.

Emerson, Lori. 2014. *Reading Writing Interfaces: From the Digital to the Bookbound*. Minneapolis: University of Minnesota Press.

Ensslin, Astrid. 2014. *Literary Gaming*. Cambridge, MA: The MIT Press.

Flores, Leonardo. 2019. "Third Generation Electronic Literature." *Electronic Book Review*. doi:10.7273/axyj-3574

Funkhouser, C. T. 2007a. "Electronic Literature circa WWW (and Before)." *Electronic Book Review*. https://electronicbookreview.com/publications/electronic-literature-circa-www-and-before/

Funkhouser, C. T. 2007b. *Prehistoric Digital Poetry: An Archaeology of Forms, 1959–1995*. Tuscaloosa, AL: The University of Alabama Press.

Gallix, Andrew. 2008. "Is E-Literature Just One Big Anti-Climax?" *The Guardian*, sec. Books. www.theguardian.com/books/booksblog/2008/sep/24/ebooks

Grigar, Dene, and Stuart Moulthrop. 2014. "Pathfinders: 25 Years of Experimental Literary Art." In *Modern Language Association 2014 Convention*, Chicago. http://dtc-wsuv.org/wp/pathfinders/exhibit/

Grigar, Dene, and Stuart Moulthrop. 2015. *Pathfinders: Documenting the Experience of Early Digital Literature*. Vancouver, WA: Nouspace Publications. http://scalar.usc.edu/works/pathfinders/index.

Grigar, Dene, and James O'Sullivan, eds. 2021. *Electronic Literature as Digital Humanities: Contexts, Forms, and Practices*. Bloomsbury Academic.

Hayles, N. Katherine. 2007. "Electronic Literature: What Is It?" *Electronic Literature Organization*. https://eliterature.org/pad/elp.html

Hayles, N. Katherine. 2008. *Electronic Literature: New Horizons for the Literary*. Notre Dame, Indiana: University of Notre Dame Press.

Heckman, Davin, and James O'Sullivan. 2018. "Electronic Literature: Contexts and Poetics." In *Literary Studies in a Digital Age*, edited by Kenneth M. Price and Ray Siemens. New York: Modern Language Association. doi:10.1632/lsda.2018.14

Jerz, Dennis G. 2007. "Somewhere Nearby Is Colossal Cave: Examining Will Crowther's Original *Adventure* in Code and in Kentucky." *Digital Humanities Quarterly* 1 (2). www.digitalhumanities.org/dhq/vol/1/2/000009/000009.html

Kac, Eduardo. 2007. *Media Poetry: An International Anthology*. Bristol and Chicago: Intellect Books.

Landow, George P. 1992. *Hypertext: The Convergence of Contemporary Critical Theory and Technology*. Baltimore: The Johns Hopkins University Press.

Maher, Jimmy. 2017. "The Eastgate School of 'Serious' Hypertext." *The Digital Antiquarian* (blog). www.filfre.net/2017/02/the-eastgate-school-of-serious-hypertext/

Manovich, Lev. 2001. *The Language of New Media*. Cambridge, MA: The MIT Press.

Montfort, Nick. 2005. *Twisty Little Passages: An Approach to Interactive Fiction*. Cambridge, MA: The MIT Press.

Morin, Roc. 2016. "Inside the Artificial Universe That Creates Itself." *The Atlantic*, February 18. www.theatlantic.com/technology/archive/2016/02/artificial-universe-no-mans-sky/463308/

Moulthrop, Stuart, and Dene Grigar. 2017. *Traversals: The Use of Preservation for Early Electronic Writing*. Cambridge, MA: The MIT Press.

O'Sullivan, James. 2017a. "Electronic Literature's Contemporary Moment: Breeze and Campbell's 'All the Delicate Duplicates'." *Los Angeles Review of Books*, November 7. https://lareviewofbooks.org/article/electronic-literature-turns-a-new-page-breeze-and-campbells-all-the-delicate-duplicates/

O'Sullivan, James. 2017b. "'The Dream of an Island': Dear Esther and the Digital Sublime." Edited by Astrid Ensslin, Pawel Frelik, and Lisa Swanstrom. *Paradoxa* 29: 313–326.

O'Sullivan, James. 2019a. "Good Literature Can Come in Digital Forms: Just Look to the World of Video Games." *The Conversation*, December 2019. https://theconversation.com/good-literature-can-come-in-digital-forms-just-look-to-the-world-of-video-games-127971

O'Sullivan, James. 2019b. "Interactivity and the Illusion of Choice." In *Towards a Digital Poetics: Electronic Literature & Literary Games*, 77–93. Palgrave Macmillan.

O'Sullivan, James. 2019c. *Towards a Digital Poetics: Electronic Literature & Literary Games*. Palgrave Macmillan.

O'Sullivan, James. 2023. "Literary Games, Walking Simulators and the New Wave of Digital Fiction." In *The Routledge Companion to Literary Media*, edited by Astrid Ensslin, Julia Round, and Thomas Bronwen, 255–267. Taylor & Francis.

O'Sullivan, James. 2024. "Starfield Is an Analogy for Our Time." *Substack* (blog). October 31. https://substack.com/home/post/p-150971806

O'Sullivan, James, and Dene Grigar. 2019. "The Origins of Electronic Literature as Net/Web Art." In *The SAGE Handbook of Web History*, edited by Niels Brügger and Ian Milligan, 428–440. Thousand Oaks, CA: SAGE.

Pawlicka, Urszula. 2014. "Towards a History of Electronic Literature." *CLCWeb: Comparative Literature and Culture* 16 (5). doi:10.7771/1481-4374.2619

Rettberg, Scott. 2010. "Editorial Process and the Idea of Genre in Electronic Literature in the Electronic Literature Collection, Volume 1." *Archiving Electronic Literature and Poetry: Problems, Tendencies, Perspectives* 29 (1/2): 85–95.

Rettberg, Scott. 2016. "Electronic Literature as Digital Humanities." In *A New Companion to Digital Humanities*, edited by Susan Schreibman, Ray Siemens, and John Unsworth, 127–136. West Sussex: John Wiley & Sons.

Rettberg, Scott. 2019. *Electronic Literature*. Cambridge and Medford, MA: Polity Press.

Rettberg, Scott, Patricia Tomaszek, and Sandy Baldwin. 2015. *Electronic Literature Communities*. Morgantown: West Virginia University Press.

Rosario, Giovanna di. 2011. *Electronic Poetry: Understanding Poetry in the Digital Environment*. Jyväskylä: University of Jyväskylä. https://jyx.jyu.fi/dspace/bitstream/handle/123456789/27117/9789513943356.pdf

Saum-Pascual, Alex, and Scott Rettberg, eds. 2020. "Electronic Literature [Frame] Works for the Creative Digital Humanities." https://electronicbookreview.com/gatherings/electronic-literature-frameworks-for-the-creative-digital-humanities/

Walker Rettberg, Jill. 2012. "Electronic Literature Seen from a Distance: The Beginnings of a Field." *Dichtung Digital: A Journal of Art and Culture in Digital Media*, 41. https://hdl.handle.net/1956/6272

Wardrip-Fruin, Noah. 2008. "Reading Digital Literature: Surface, Data, Interaction, and Expressive Processing." In *A Companion to Digital Literary Studies*, edited by Susan Schreibman and Ray Siemens, 163–182. Oxford: Blackwell.

5

DIGITAL PUBLISHING

The National Library of Ireland can be found on Kildare Street in Dublin, a striking feat of classical architecture[1] set among such landmarks as Leinster House, the country's seat of parliament, and the archaeological branch of the National Museum. The library often exhibits materials from its many collections, the nonpareil of which is arguably their permanent exhibition on the famed author W. B. Yeats, called *The Life and Work of William Butler Yeats*, which first opened to the public in 2006. Based on the library's renowned collection of Yeats manuscripts, the largest such collection in the world, the exhibition has achieved critical acclaim and numerous accolades. What is also noteworthy about the exhibition is its virtual tour, which has photographed the space so that the physical experience might be recreated as faithfully as possible for visitors who cannot attend in person. The virtual tour does not just provide access to the materials, it seeks to replicate the physical exhibition so that its staging and spatiality are retained for those experiencing the various installations and displays through a screen.

This exhibition demonstrates both the promise and the peril of digital publishing in the humanities. While the virtual tour

DOI: 10.4324/9781351203395-5

extends access beyond geographic boundaries, its original Flash-based platform now serves as a cautionary tale about digital preservation. Robust approaches to digital publishing tend to balance a number of imperatives: leveraging technology's affordances for enhanced access and engagement, ensuring long-term preservation of cultural materials, and maintaining equitable distribution of knowledge. Scholarly publishing's future depends on developing sustainable models that honour the strengths of both print and digital forms.

When we speak of digital publishing, there is still, among so many, a tendency to think about the most basic acts of textual remediation, WordPress blog posts and Kindle e-books. But digital publishing offers so much more than just text on a screen, it offers, as evidenced by the National Library of Ireland's Yeats exhibitions, a chance to imitate the physical in ways which greatly diminishes the impact of distance between objects and their viewers. Yet this promise comes with significant challenges. The exhibition shows how digital publishing is not about re-formatting for the sake of distribution; digital publishing is all about reciprocity, about making something physical wholly or partially digital, while also bringing the digital into physical spaces, and vice versa.

These are simple notions with radical potential, and fortunately for the consumers of culture, they are now so commonplace among cultural institutions that portals like Google Arts & Culture have emerged, allowing the public to explore and experience a great many museums, galleries and cultural spaces using a myriad of immersive techniques and technologies. But the Yeats exhibition, first developed using Adobe's dying Flash platform, also provides a cautionary tale. The exhibition's current inaccessibility due to Flash's deprecation illustrates a fundamental tension in digital publishing, that the very technologies that enable innovative access can also threaten long-term preservation. How do we balance innovation with sustainability? What happens to our digital cultural heritage when platforms become obsolete? There is much in corporeal material and spaces that the digital cannot reliably mimic, particularly those qualities of composition which have allowed many cultural artifacts to endure hundreds, even thousands of years. Physical media like the page last, they outlast the rise and fall of platforms; if one can get to them, they can experience them as intended, without interference by the many variables introduced by computers and their applications.

Publishing is principally about sharing, about formalising the production of content so that it can be disseminated and consumed. In this, the digital has much to offer, and not just at the grand scale of a virtualised museum, but also with the plaintext e-book type material which is, however comparatively humdrum, still hugely important to society and culture. Publishing should also be about preservation, not necessarily always, but often enough that those using digital tools and platforms for the dissemination of culture and knowledge should be conscious of the obsolescence which looms over many electronic formats. And so digital publishing is really about two things: using technologies to share content, ideally, in a way that makes use of the affordances of the screen, and making sure that whatever is published exists well beyond the life of its creators. These two pursuits, certainly the first one, seem like simple enough endeavours, but the question of *how* one shares culture has never been so problematic. This tension between innovation and preservation runs throughout digital publishing initiatives.

Bringing together experts from the humanities, information sciences, and computing, the digital humanities have an important role to play in answering such questions. The words of Mark Sample, cited in a previous chapter, are relevant once more:

> The promise of the digital is not in the way it allows us to ask new questions because of digital tools or because of new methodologies made possible by those tools. The promise is in the way the digital reshapes the representation, sharing, and discussion of knowledge. We are no longer bound by the physical demands of printed books and paper journals, no longer constrained by production costs and distribution friction, no longer hampered by a top-down and unsustainable business model. And we should no longer be content to make our work public achingly slowly along ingrained routes, authors and readers alike delayed by innumerable gateways limiting knowledge production and sharing.
>
> (Sample 2013, 256)

Sample's optimism, however, requires critical examination. While digital publishing may remove some barriers, it creates others—technological, economic, and cultural—that we must acknowledge. There are many scholars who would reject Sample's assertion that the real promise of the digital lies in the representation, sharing, and discussion of knowledge rather than in the digital tools and methods that allow us to ask new questions through distant reading. Any tool or technique that allows us to look at culture and its products in new and different ways holds much promise. But whatever his take on DH of the analytical sort, there is something to Sample's position. While it may be a step too far to suggest that sharing is the real promise of the digital, how knowledge is represented and disseminated is hugely important and deeply relevant to the arts and humanities.

Therefore, it is easy to see why so many in DH occupy their time with exploring the various ways in which the digital allows us to challenge and even break the norms of diffusion in the arts and humanities. As also noted in Chapter 2, when configured in the context of sharing, there are strong associations between the digital and the public humanities. Sample's provocation suggests that the principles of the public humanities should be an inherent part of anyone's DH, and perhaps that is already the case: scholars who care only about distant reading and analysis, and not one bit about publishing models and issues of access, still give great consideration to the consumption of the knowledge they are creating. Whenever one chooses to represent analytical findings using graphic illustrations, when one chooses visualisation over some other means of communication, they are giving thought to how their readers, however many or few, will engage with their message. One cannot separate knowledge production from consumption, because any act of publishing implies thinking about audience (Blanke et al. 2014, 26).

Maybe there are no digital humanities without the public humanities. Moreover, one could argue that any sharing in the contemporary context, whatever the domain, needs the digital. It would be far more useful to turn attention to the things that scholars of DH are doing in this domain, how they are using the digital to perform the kinds of reshaping of knowledge so essential to the present and future of the consumption of cultural knowledge.

DIGITAL MERCHANTS OF CULTURE

Publishers have been described as "merchants of culture," as hybrid creatures "one part star gazer, one part gambler, one part businessman, one part midwife and three parts optimist" (Bhaskar 2013, 1). Digital humanities is full of these star gazers and gamblers, backing that next new thing to bring about some genuine evolution; business types, seeking models to fund digital initiatives; and optimists, believing that the cause of digital publishing is mostly to the betterment of culture and society. But what happens when these roles conflict?

These digital merchants of culture pursue "the new possibilities of digital publishing" (Blanke et al. 2014, 25), they think explicitly about the role of computers in connecting the producers of knowledge and meaning with consumers. And the challenge in that, as already noted, is ensuring that the affordances of the screen are properly utilised, otherwise, what is the point? For the digital humanities to be something other, then it needs to offer something new. As Blanke, Pierazzo, and Stokes put it in their useful account of digital publishing in the contest of DH, publishing in this context "has to mean more than relying on faithful reproductions" (Blanke et al. 2014, 26).

This is an interesting perspective, because reproduction can serve political ideals, most notably preservation and access that are considered central to the humanities. Publishing is not just about text, it is also, as addressed by Blanke, Pierazzo, and Stokes, about more complex objects, the reproduction of which requires extensive expertise in matters of representation and history. The degree to which a complex object has been "faithfully" reproduced is often a subjective matter, and where reproduction requires such interpretation, it is good to include the digital humanities, experts who appreciate both the thing being reproduced and the technologies of reproduction. Faithful reproduction, however banal, plays a hugely important role in the preservation of cultural heritage, in the provision of access to objects and materials which would otherwise remain hidden from view for so many. This raises a critical question: who decides what constitutes "faithful" reproduction, and whose cultural heritage is prioritised in these decisions?

But it is hard to disagree outright with the perspective of Blanke and his co-authors, because there are so many examples of the banality, reproductions which do nothing more than bring content to screens in static, ill-considered forms. Public engagement and the communication of scholarship can often be confused for scholarship, and while there is value in the former, there is a world of difference between blogging, posting, word clouds and websites, and the creation of real, insightful meaning. All the aforementioned activities are important for a new scholarship that allows for exchange and interchange between the marginalised and the mainstream, but such should not be the priority. Academics should be scholars first, merchants second. And so, before anything is shared in any form, the question needs to be asked, why? Why this, why digital? Again, it all comes back to intention.

Preservation and access alone are not sufficient justification for digital endeavours: print, unlike links, never breaks, so is far superior to any form of digital preservation, and access should only be desired when there is value in that which has been made accessible. Even from an economic perspective, the cost of accessing certain print resources can be less daunting than their digital surrogates, the price of which cannot be isolated from the devices, infrastructures, and digital literacies on which they are reliant. If living through a global pandemic has taught us anything, it is that the digital divide, even in supposedly wealthy regions, has never been wider. The COVID-19 pandemic exposed how digital publishing's promise of universal access remains unfulfilled when basic technological infrastructure is unevenly distributed, a reality check which forces us to reconsider Sample's optimistic vision. Despite all the star gazers and the disruptive potential in new technologies, the structures of power and the broader social relations which have long defined publishing and its environs have not radically changed in the digital age (Thompson 2012, vii). If anything, the influence of a very small few agents has only been extended.

But none of this means that the optimists should quit, and DH scholars concerned with the dynamics of publishing should never stop seeking to remedy the many failings in how we reproduce and share knowledge and culture. They should not stop because there have been some successes, both in the development of many new infrastructures and platforms, and in smaller, independent uses of digital tools to allow liberation from some of the material confines of the paper-based page. Large-scale digital publishing projects that have been pursued partly under the DH banner, or are led by scholars who self-identify as being part of the DH community, include the Open Library of Humanities, the Humanities Commons (now Knowledge Commons), Omeka, and Scalar. Each represents a different approach to the challenges outlined above; the Open Library of Humanities addresses economic barriers through diamond open access, Humanities Commons tackles the problem of scholarly networking beyond commercial platforms, while Omeka and Scalar provide alternatives to proprietary content management systems. Their varying degrees of success offer important lessons. Each of these projects and platforms does something that cannot be achieved without the digital, and each has been developed for the humanities. There are often unforeseen and unintended consequences when humanities scholars are forced to use commercial, catch-all solutions to distribute their ideas. Some of these consequences can be minor, some of them, such as surveillance, are more troubling. For instance, when scholars use Academia.edu or ResearchGate, they trade access for data, contributing to surveillance capitalism's expansion into academic life. Such consequences can be greatly diminished through the availability of digital publishing tools that have been developed specifically for the humanities with funding from transparent, public sources. While many of these platforms are relatively fledgling resources, their efficacy in matters of access, community-building, and the dissemination of culture and knowledge is being thoroughly examined and justified (Eve 2013b; Eve et al. 2017), while scholars are also asking how digital tools might now allow us to reimagine practices like peer review, authorship, and crowdsourcing (Fitzpatrick 2012; Risam 2014; Nyhan and Duke-Williams 2014; Terras 2016).

Major projects which provide publishing platforms and infrastructures upon which scholars and practitioners might build in the service of the humanities are hugely important, but they should not be allowed to overshadow innovative acts of digital publishing which emerge out of smaller, subject specific independent research projects, because it is through the latter that we access the new knowledge that publishing is designed to support. The distinction here is crucial: infrastructure projects enable publishing, while content projects demonstrate what digital publishing can achieve when properly conceived. Any act of digital publishing will, ideally, use a model that can be easily replicated elsewhere, but the main concern should be whether or not the use of digital media enabled sharing of the sort that would not have otherwise been possible. Such a query allows us to distinguish between thoughtless reproduction and DH as DH is meant to be done, purposeful and in the service of scholarship. Again, there are many examples, critical digital publishing projects like *Poetics of the Archive*, *The Modernist Archives Publishing Project*, the *Baudelaire Song Project*, and *Pathfinders*, each of which shows how the digital can be used to produce scholarly resources heavily reliant on paratextual materials and multimodal content unsuited to print publication. What unites these projects is their recognition that digital publishing must do more than replicate print. *Pathfinders* preserves early electronic literature through video documentation of users interacting with obsolete systems, capturing experiential knowledge that no print description could convey. The unsuitability of print is why these projects are digital, but it is their critical value, the intentional way in which their investigators connect the resource to new insights and cultural understanding, that makes them DH. Of particular value to this current discussion is the book which accompanies *The Modernist Archives Publishing Project* (Battershill et al. 2017), wherein the authors reflect on the building of their critical digital archive as an act of public scholarship.

Well considered projects of this sort come about when DH scholars and practitioners heed the warnings of Quinn Dombrowski and "don't leap into buying a pony" (Dombrowski 2019). They think, like any good merchant should, about the thing that they are trading, and how it should be brought to its consumers. Culture is a strange commodity, in that those who trade in it tend to care very much about its exchange and future. With the digital increasingly fetishised and incessant sharing an active part of the human condition, it can be easy for the merchants of culture to focus too much on the modes of distribution and far too little on the idea, knowledge, or heritage being dispersed. The digital merchants of culture need to take a breath, ask what they are sharing, why they are sharing it, who will consume it, and most importantly in this context, what the digital brings, not in some lofty, general sense, but specifically, if anything, to that process.

ON AN OPEN HUMANITIES

When examining digital publishing and the digital humanities, or indeed, digital publishing in any disciplinary context, one cannot neglect the matter of open access. Open access is *the* great promise of digital publishing, and so it is surprising to see that, still, the humanities are moving towards open access at a far slower pace than the sciences (Suber 2017). This disparity reveals deeper structural issues about how different forms of knowledge are valued in our society. It has been over twenty years since Peter Suber outlined why the humanities have been experiencing a slower permeation of open access principles when compared with the sciences, suggesting that "it is less urgent and harder to subsidize than in the sciences" (Suber 2005). Little has changed in the interim. A lack of urgency on the part of funding agencies and policymakers is merely a reflection of how the humanities are held in the public imagination: cultural knowledge is simply not a priority. It is easy for cash rich disciplines to be more open than those which struggle for resources. This is a regrettable reality but a reality, nonetheless. But scholars and practitioners in the arts and humanities must also be held accountable, because they too have shown a lack of urgency when it comes to broad adoption of the open agenda.

This want of haste is perhaps surprising considering the stated commitments to values of equality and social betterment than one typically encounters in the humanities. "To benefit from someone's research, we need access to it, and for this purpose it doesn't matter whether the research is in the sciences or humanities," writes Suber (2012, 114). This is a simple idea, and shows why policymakers, who think all the benefit is to be found in scientific and technical disciplines, neglect the arts and humanities. What is curious is why so many scholars in the latter also seem content for access to their work to be severely restricted; do they also think it of limited benefit? This question cuts to the heart of a troubling possibility: have humanities scholars internalised the very devaluation of their work that they claim to resist? Scholars in the arts and humanities have as much to gain from open access as their counterparts in the sciences (Terras 2012)—access promotes originality, reproducibility; it allows scholars to enter into a reciprocal exchange of mutually beneficial interpretations, facts, and materials (Eve 2014, 22). And more importantly, it allows the public to benefit from the kinds of essential knowledge created by scholars in the arts and humanities.

A lot of good things have been said about open access, most notably, that it promotes equality in education and in access to knowledge. Suber has written a comprehensive treatment of the open access movement (Suber 2012), while Martin Paul Eve, who co-founded the Open Library of Humanities alongside Caroline Edwards, penned an extensive examination of open access in the context of the humanities (Eve 2014). Few outwardly disagree with Suber and Eve when they lend support to the movement, and it is not that the ideals of open access go unpronounced within the arts and humanities, but that is still relatively rare to see, with some notable exceptions aside, such pronouncements manifested as something more tangible. The gap between rhetorical support and practical implementation suggests that deeper structural barriers exist. A myriad of institutional and cultural limitations must be overcome before everyone is convinced that open is the way forward, and furthermore, the very notion of openness needs to be routinely problematised in the context of our increasingly neoliberal world, but the fact remains that the collective appetite necessary for a truly open humanities to be accomplished is just not there. Why?

Part of the resistance that open access faces in the humanities comes from many scholars and practitioners feeling as though "they are having openness violently thrust upon them" (Eve 2013a). This perception of coercion reflects legitimate concerns about academic autonomy and the commodification of scholarly communication. It is possible that this sense of coercion is connected to the rise of the digital humanities, and it can be hard for communities of practice to accept an awful lot of change in a short amount of time. A few decades ago, most people had not even heard of DH, and now it has its own programmes and departments, drawing its share of the resources from what is already a very shallow well. As DH has risen, so too has digital publishing, so it is natural that they might be lumped together by anyone who might be frustrated by either.

The DH community is making substantial contributions to the open access movement, but open access is a transdisciplinary matter, and the challenges that openness presents for the humanities are shared by the digital humanities. One could reasonably argue that at least half of the most respected journals, and indeed, most of the monographs and edited collections in DH, are not published as open access. This hypocrisy undermines DH's claims to transformative practice. How can we advocate for open access while continuing to perpetuate closed systems? Many of the cultural materials studied by DH scholars, even those using distant reading methods, are not open access. Some even conduct these analyses using tools and platforms that are extremely expensive, proprietary systems. It is possible that DH scholars are generally more sympathetic to the open movement than are their counterparts in the traditional humanities, but only a few of them act upon this sentiment. Exploring the notion of an open humanities is not about making the wider humanities more digital, it is about seeing whether or not we might ever achieve a truly open humanities *and* open digital humanities.

But what does it even mean to be open? This question requires careful unpacking, as "openness" has become a contested term, often co-opted by commercial interests. Openness first entered scholarly vocabulary as a synonym for "free," the idea that publications should be placed in venues where they can be accessed by anyone at any time. It has since extended, particularly in the digital humanities, to include the broader set of materials needed to develop knowledge, such as datasets and primary sources; there are earlier print precedents for this logic too, where monographs direct readers via notes to the full empirical materials underpinning their conclusions. Scholars in the arts and humanities have long privileged the "end products" of research, giving their interpretations away but denying others access to the materials from which such interpretations are drawn. Most scholars now recognise the need to not only provide access to traditional outputs like papers and books, but also, where morally and legally permissible, the materials and tools from which they have constructed their arguments. Such an open view of sharing requires a fundamental shift in how labour is valued in the arts and humanities, because nobody wants to admit that their dataset is, in the eyes of their peers, more valuable than their paper or book and the many great insights contained within. This hierarchy of value reflects deeper assumptions about what constitutes "real" scholarship, assumptions that digital humanities must challenge if it is to fulfil its transformative potential.

For a truly open humanities to be achieved, different kinds of labour would need to be equally acknowledged. Scholars who skilfully expose important cultural narratives from sources would continue to be celebrated and we should never stop cherishing those who can take masses of information and craft a story that teaches us something about our humanity. But we would also hail the efforts of those who curated the archive or compiled the information, experts who provided access to such sources so that everyone can experience such origins for themselves without the intervention of some third-party perspective. To be truly open the humanities need to give everything away, not just the polished treatise that comes at the end, and right now there is no incentive for anyone to do that, because it is unacknowledged labour that simply will not progress a career. A scholar in the arts and humanities who wants to make a name for themselves produces books and journal articles, not datasets. This creates a vicious cycle: datasets remain closed because they are undervalued, and they remain undervalued partly because their visibility and citability are limited. There are, of course, precedents in print culture, but such practices have tended to be exceptional rather than routine. What digital infrastructures alter is the scale and standardisation with which underlying research materials can be transparently shared.

Again, fear is a motivating factor: keeping one's sources hidden away ensures control over the research narrative because there can only be one. Preventing research materials from being openly accessible serves scholarly self-interests, building capital and prestige with research outputs which act as the only real means through which others can experience the thing that is locked away. Something which is truly open is available in its entirety, rather than as a strategic selection of fragments designed to maintain, even in some small way, the control of a piece of knowledge and its origins. There will always be some reason to retain a measure of control, and scholars cannot be expected to produce research using materials which cannot be openly shared when the reality is that many valuable sources of cultural understanding remain bound by a range of legal, moral, and cultural constraints, and so a balance must be sought between research which is intentionally restricted for self-serving purposes, and research which is open in the truest sense. In recent years that balance has come to be known as FAIR, which advocates for findability, accessibility, interoperability, and reusability (Wilkinson et al. 2016). FAIR principles offer a pragmatic middle ground, but their implementation in humanities contexts raises specific challenges that deserve examination.

We may never realise a truly open arts and humanities, but we might yet achieve some fairness. Maria Cruz used the 2019 CERN-UNIGE Workshop on Innovations in Scholarly Communication as an opportunity to demonstrate how a lack of awareness among researchers was one of the major barriers to the adoption of FAIR principles (Cruz 2019). But awareness alone will remain insufficient as long as promotion systems do not reward data sharing, funding models do not support long-term preservation, and technical infrastructures make FAIR compliance difficult. As such awareness permeates the arts and humanities, perhaps we will see an increasing shift away from publishing as an inherently selfish undertaking. "Selfish" may seem too strong a word, and many scholars would argue vehemently that they publish in the name of knowledge, but we do so in exchange for cultural capital; science is not done for the benefit of science, it is done for the benefit of scientists, or so the adage goes. At the very least, FAIR principles privilege the interests of communities and publics over narrow self-interests, however effaced such self-interest might be. There are encouraging signs that some DH scholars are trying to be FAIR (Murphy and Egan 2023). Publications like the *Journal of Cultural Analytics*, for example, facilitate essays which link to replication data (Underwood et al. 2018), or the *Journal of Open Humanities Data* and its exemplary "data articles," a section of the journal which allows authors to submit descriptions of datasets for peer-review and publication. These examples demonstrate that alternative models are possible, but they remain exceptions rather than the rule.

It is not always easy to be FAIR when one is a scholar in a discipline routinely deprecated by those making decisions on funding and resource allocation. The monograph is still central to the humanities, and that is a good thing, because it presents sustained, long-form and in-depth arguments, demonstrating mastery in a way that is difficult to replicate through other forms of scholarly output. And monographs, unlike papers and articles, are more difficult to accommodate using open access models, while sometimes they are just neglected by institutional investment in open infrastructures designed for shorter forms. The monograph problem exemplifies how open access models developed for the sciences do not translate easily to humanities contexts. Great strides are being made (Penier et al. 2020), but there are still a number of hurdles to be overcome before it is feasible for open access monographs to be commonplace in the humanities. There are still concerns over cost and technical interoperability (Hill 2020). There are still concerns over how the publishing industry, and its many, small university and independent presses that are often hidden in the shadow of larger conglomerates, will adapt to this changing world. Not everyone will have the funds or expertise available to simply adapt their business models and upskill staff (Alexander 2014). Admittedly, some small publishing enterprises are, to cite Eve, "seizing the bull by the horns," trialling various ways through which they might "openly disseminate work that would otherwise remain accessible to a relatively privileged few," or more pragmatically, simply figuring out how "to salvage their business models" in an increasingly paperless world (Eve 2013a).

Some people just prefer print, and that is fine. Printed knowledge has sustained itself for hundreds of years, and print monographs are beautiful, they are real, tactile things. As the publisher Patrick Alexander puts it: "Books have an aesthetic above and beyond what's between the boards" (Alexander 2014). One cannot simply dismiss the centrality of print to the humanities as antiquated thinking, because print has so much aesthetic and material value, and real, viable alternatives are still being worked out. The demand for print might never wane, no matter how digital the humanities or publishing become. Resistance to open access is not always profit motivated, it is sometimes ideological, borne of a belief in print as opposed to a rejection of the digital. One can believe in both.

But say the rejection of open access is profit motivated, what then? It can be galling to think of large corporations making financial gains from research produced at public institutions, and yes, open access is an antidote to the extortionate catalogue fees charged by some publishers. Individual authors are an entirely different matter, and it is difficult to see why anyone might object to a scholar profiting from the sale of their book. The position that individual scholars, wherever and however they are employed, should forego all intellectual property because they might be paid, in whole or in part, by the exchequer, seems terribly draconian. This argument becomes more complex when we consider how individual profit motives can conflict with collective benefit. It is only in the rarest of cases that a scholar in the humanities would make a substantial profit from the royalties on a manuscript, but even if their annual income amounts to only a few cents, it really is a matter of principle. First, in a time of tax breaks and business incentives, there are very few workers on this earth who can claim to earn income that is entirely free of some state contribution. But more importantly, the perspective that the authors of books should not be allowed to monetise their intellectual property because they are simultaneously contracted to a public or semi-public institution makes a dangerous and sweeping assumption about the individuals who work in research and education. There are many staff at institutes of education working on precarious contracts, there are many who come from working class backgrounds, there are many who are contracted only to teach, and research is not seen as part of their job and something to be done in their own time. Applying blanket suppositions to all public workers with regard to intellectual property is completely ignorant of the dynamics of labour. The idea of property and ownership is central to most contemporary societies, so it would seem strange to think that scholars and the writers of books should be expected to live outside such conventions.

Jaron Lanier argues in *Who Owns the Future?* that digital platforms only serve to further the concentration of wealth (Lanier 2014). Organisations like Google, to take one of many examples, generate massive profits from user-generated content for which they pay no remuneration. While open access resources might not be directly connected to Google, their search engine only works in an ecosystem where there is a lot of content for users to sift through: the more digital content that people create, the more giants like Google will benefit. Whenever someone produces free digital content, they are causing searches from which Google can profit, more traffic for Google to mine and more users for Google to act upon, a transaction from which that original creator receives no monetary gain. By encouraging individuals to give away their intellectual property for free, but also allowing platform providers like Google to profit from that labour, we are laying the foundation for a future owned by a very select cohort. This paradox, that open access can simultaneously democratise knowledge and concentrate power, remains unresolved in current OA models.

Arguments pertaining to open access often appear visceral: its proponents sometimes fail to acknowledge the rights of authors and the realities of publishing, or indeed, the institutions and power dynamics within which scholars are forced to operate, while its detractors cite the aforementioned barriers with such ferocity that one would think the pursuit of alternative models and structures through which they might protect and share their intellectual property is an inconceivable task.

A measure of admiration is owed to those individuals who have created something of monetary value and decided to share this with the world in a way that potentially limits their ability to capitalise on that worth. This admiration should not be reserved for products with palpable commercial prospects; a humanities scholar who chooses to commit their knowledge to an open platform rather than print, considering the latter largely remains the currency of many fields, has sacrificed as much as the software developer who releases a tool for free. A real sense of open access cannot be acquired through a detached analysis from the fringes. One needs to face the pragmatic and intellectual repercussions that openness might have for their own creations and careers, forming an impression right there in the mire.[2]

The digital divide is such that open access can never be implemented with absolute equivalence, but it is, at the very least, more equal than alternative models: "Priced access is stratified and unequal access" (Suber 2013). This alone is possibly sufficient justification of the open access agenda, and why we should strive for a more open, and thus more equal, arts and humanities. This is not to say that we should refrain from challenging the ideals of the movement, but if the humanities are to be a vehicle for economic improvement and social inclusion, if the humanities are to be for all humanity, we need at the very least to examine with real conviction the extent to which open digital publishing can liberate knowledge and ideas from the disseminative models which only serve to constrain.

THE FUTURE OF PUBLISHING

There have been a great many things heralded as the future of publishing: CD-ROMs, e-books, mobile apps, a battery of social media platforms, audiobooks, virtual and augmented, and all those little-known devices that went hurriedly from the fanfare of release to the museum of obsolete technologies. However long a list someone may care to devise, nothing detailed will have survived nearly as long as print. That is because print just works; it has worked, both materially and economically, since its first inception, and it has long satisfied the requirements of those looking to share knowledge and ideas in intuitive, sustainable forms. Unlike the digital and its many features, models, and links, print never breaks. This durability offers a crucial lesson: any digital future must learn from print's strengths rather than simply trying to supersede them. That print continues to thrive in this digital age proves its qualities as an instrument for publishing, but it also shows how print is increasingly seen as an antidote to the omnipresence of screens in our lives (Pressman 2020). Print has an essential role to play in a digital culture that threatens to consume us all.

But just because print continues to endure does not mean that there is no room for other publishing technologies, and the future of publishing, as it is at present, will hopefully be one in which many ways of sharing co-exist. Reaching that future will require compromise: some will have to accept that print will be with us for a long time yet, while others will have to recognise that new forms also have value. More importantly, we must move beyond the false binary of print versus digital to consider how each medium's affordances can complement the other. Dichotomies between print and digital, steadfast views that all sharing should conform to certain ideals and standards, will need to dissolve if the future of publishing is to be the brightest possible. Beyond ideological perspectives, there is also a need to reach consensus on how best to facilitate new units of scholarly publication (Burton et al. 2019), how to fix outmoded models of print publishing, and how to make the most of genuinely promising new technologies. The future of publishing, both print and digital, has much to benefit from everyone taking a pause to consider how we should best progress.[3] Naysayers of all persuasions need to start accepting that the creators of content know what form is best for publishing their work, but creators also need to be honest with themselves and really justify *how* something should be shared, not just why. If everyone started doing this—really started doing it—that would make for a more promising future.

Right now, it seems as though, certainly, as far as digital publishing is concerned, we are doomed to repeat the mistakes of the past. The recurring cycle of hype, adoption, obsolescence, and abandonment suggests we haven't learned the fundamental lessons about sustainable digital infrastructure. It is evident from a brief survey of the field that the lessons DH scholars like Dombrowski are trying to teach are going unheeded:

> When starting a project, think hard about how long you want to personally be responsible for maintaining infrastructure—not just given your life today, but how it might be different in two years or five years from now.... What are the dependencies for your project to keep running in the form you plan to create it in? What other forms can it meaningfully exist in, in the longer term? How much work will it take to adapt it to that form? Would it be better for you to start the project in that form? What is your exit strategy when the time comes for you to step away? (Your answer should not involve someone else coming along to keep the project going; it's not impossible, but it is highly improbable, even for projects with a large following.)
>
> (Dombrowski 2019)

Dombrowski's questions cut to the heart of digital publishing's sustainability crisis. Too often, projects are conceived in terms of launch rather than lifecycle, innovation rather than maintenance. Everyone within the wider arts and humanities need to start recognising when they are being duped. Dead links are all that gets returned from digital projects that are not fully considered—the DH mausoleum is full enough with dead ambitions, and we have all built enough personal monuments to failure.

Personal responsibility is important, and if we are to continue to wrap ideas and their dissemination in digital frameworks, "we must be as mindful of the dangers as we are of the opportunities, being as critical of the screen as we have been of the page, so that the repercussions of any transformation in the transaction between creator and receiver are fully comprehended and expressed" (O'Sullivan et al. 2016, 386). As we continue to share through digital platforms, we extend the reach of knowledge and create possibilities for the cultivation of the self and the curation of communities of praxis independent of place, but we also enter in panopticon-like structures where ethical and moral scrutiny is vital (Kim 2014). The surveillance inherent in digital platforms raises questions about academic freedom and intellectual privacy that the field has yet to adequately address.

But it is not all bad, and there already exists many laudable exemplars—a few of which were noted earlier in this chapter—for what the future of publishing might look like, DH projects where the digital is used to share knowledge and ideas that, if produced in print, would have been compromised. There are many projects which have been built on sustainable platforms, and have considered the ethics of publishing, both in terms of the new challenges presented by the digital, and those challenges that have persisted since the rise of the practice. There are many publishing projects where the essential suitability of the chosen form is undeniably clear. The future of publishing, particularly the future of digital publishing, needs to mimic such exemplars. But mimicry alone is insufficient; we need principles that can guide future development.

Also, more should be done with emerging technologies, particularly in areas like augmented and virtual reality, and 3D printing, where relatively affordable devices are now making their way to market. Projects like *Joycestick*, developed by Joseph Nugent and a team of students at Boston College, allow readers to experience the setting for a piece of literature through virtual reality (Hanel 2017), while 3D modelling initiatives like Scan the World[4] allow for important cultural artefacts and sculptures to be reproduced anywhere, by anyone, using 3D printers. These projects suggest possibilities beyond text, but they also raise familiar questions about preservation, access, and the digital divide. How do we ensure VR experiences remain accessible when hardware becomes obsolete? Who benefits from 3D printing of cultural artefacts, and who controls the files? Whatever the future of publishing might be, there should be room in that future for sharing of this sort, sharing that is immersive, sharing that allows for things other than text to be replicated and reproduced.

The future of publishing might not be very different to the present and past, and we need to be prepared to be accepting of that—some of the old ways need deconstruction, but some of the old ways work very well. The cultural conversation that surrounds digital publishing is often associated with the idea of a public humanities, which can at times seem quite amorphous. There are branches within the humanities which have a long lineage of thinking explicitly and for very reasonable purposes about the ways in which scholarship engages with the public, public history being the most obvious example. And other fields should follow suit, but not merely as an attempt to justify the humanities in the minds of policymakers and the parents of would-be enrolments. If digital publishing is to have a meaningful future, it cannot be allowed to be dragged into the realm of marketing, and any project which seeks to disseminate using the digital must do so with the intention that has been heralded as so important to DH throughout this book. It is through such intention that digital publishing, like any other activity within DH, will achieve its potential. Without intention, we will have nothing but social media posts and empty webpages, broken links and an ongoing, fruitless contest between print and screens.

The future of digital publishing in DH requires us to move beyond technological determinism toward a more nuanced understanding of how different media serve different purposes. Success will come not from choosing sides in the print/digital divide, but from developing sustainable, equitable models that leverage each medium's strengths while acknowledging their limitations. The fundamental thing is that our publishing practices align with the humanistic values we claim to uphold: accessibility, preservation, and the democratisation of knowledge. Only then can digital publishing fulfil its transformative potential without sacrificing the qualities that make humanities scholarship valuable in the first place.

RECOMMENDED READING

Bhaskar, Michael. 2013. *The Content Machine: Towards a Theory of Publishing from the Printing Press to the Digital Network*. Anthem Press.

Blanke, Tobias, Elena Pierazzo, and Peter A. Stokes. 2014. "Digital Publishing Seen from the Digital Humanities." *Logos*, 25 (2): 16–27.

Eve, Martin Paul. 2014. *Open Access and the Humanities: Contexts, Controversies and the Future*. Cambridge: Cambridge University Press. https://www.cambridge.org/core/books/open-access-and-the-humanities/02BD7DB4A5172A864C432DBFD86E5FB4

Eve, Martin Paul, and Jonathan Gray, eds. 2020. *Reassembling Scholarly Communications: Histories, Infrastructures, and Global Politics of Open Access*. The MIT Press.

Fitzpatrick, Kathleen. 2011. *Planned Obsolescence: Publishing, Technology, and the Future of the Academy*. New York: NYU Press.

Murphy, Órla, and Patrick Egan. 2023. "Sharing as CARE and FAIR in the Digital Humanities." In *The Bloomsbury Handbook to the Digital Humanities*, edited by James O'Sullivan, 267–271. London: Bloomsbury Academic. https://hdl.handle.net/10468/14776

Sample, Mark. 2013. "The Digital Humanities Is Not about Building, It's about Sharing." In *Defining Digital Humanities: A Reader*, edited by Melissa Terras, Julianne Nyhan, and Edward Vanhoutte, 255–257. Ashgate.

NOTES

1 The building was designed by Corkonian, Thomas Newenham Deane.

2 This may seem like a pointlessly antagonistic commentary, but I have spent a considerable amount of time debating the merits of open access with the most devout of acolytes, who have themselves refrained from sharing their work freely. Others should mimic scholars like Suber and Eve and lead by example, producing open work as opposed to just advocating for such.

3 An example of such essential critical reflection can be found in a recent collection edited by Martin Paul Eve and Jonathan Gray: *Reassembling Scholarly Communications: Histories, Infrastructures, and Global Politics of Open Access* (The MIT Press, 2020).

4 See myminifactory.com/scantheworld

REFERENCES

Alexander, Patrick H. 2014. "Teaching an Old University Press Publisher New Tricks: Living in the Present and Preparing for the Future of Scholarly Communications." *Journal of Electronic Publishing* 17 (2). doi:10.3998/3336451.0017.202

Battershill, Claire, Helen Southworth, Alice Staveley, Michael Widner, Elizabeth Willson Gordon, and Nicola Wilson. 2017. *Scholarly Adventures in Digital Humanities: Making The Modernist Archives Publishing Project*. Palgrave Macmillan.

Bhaskar, Michael. 2013. *The Content Machine: Towards a Theory of Publishing from the Printing Press to the Digital Network*. London and New York: Anthem Press.

Blanke, Tobias, Elena Pierazzo, and Peter A. Stokes. 2014. "Digital Publishing Seen from the Digital Humanities." *Logos* 25 (2): 16–27.

Burton, Matt, Matthew J. Lavin, Jessica Otis, and Scott B. Weingart. 2019. "Digits: Two Reports on New Units of Scholarly Publication." *Journal of Electronic Publishing* 22 (1). doi:10.3998/3336451.0022.105

Cruz, Maria. 2019. "Bringing Researchers Along on the Road to FAIR Data." Presented at the OAI 11: The CERN-UNIGE Workshop on Innovations in Scholarly Communication, June 19. doi:10.5281/zenodo.3249802

Dombrowski, Quinn. 2019. "Sorry for All the Drupal: Reflections on the 3rd Anniversary of 'Drupal for Humanists.'" Quinndombrowski.Com (blog). http://quinndombrowski.com/?q=blog/2019/11/08/sorry-all-drupal-reflections-3rd-anniversary-drupal-humanists

Eve, Martin Paul. 2013a. "Open Access and the Humanities: Reimagining Our Future." *The Guardian*, March 25, sec. Higher Education Network. www.theguardian.com/higher-education-network/blog/2013/mar/25/open-access-humanities-future

Eve, Martin Paul. 2013b. "Open Library of Humanities: A Community-Grounded Approach to Academic Publishing." LSE Impact Blog. http://blogs.lse.ac.uk/impactofsocialsciences

Eve, Martin Paul. 2014. *Open Access and the Humanities: Contexts, Controversies and the Future*. Cambridge: Cambridge University Press. https://www.cambridge.org/core/books/open-access-and-the-humanities/02BD7DB4A5172A864C432DBFD86E5FB4

Eve, Martin Paul, Saskia C. J. De Vries, and Johan Rooryck. 2017. "The Transition to Open Access: The State of the Market, Offsetting Deals, and a Demonstrated Model for Fair Open Access with the Open Library of Humanities." In *Expanding Perspectives on Open Science: Communities, Cultures and Diversity in Concepts and Practices*, edited by Leslie Chan and Fernando Loizides, 118–128. IOS Press. doi:10.3233/978-1-61499-769-6-118

Fitzpatrick, Kathleen. 2012. "Beyond Metrics: Community Authorization and Open Peer Review." In *Debates in the Digital Humanities*, edited by Matthew K. Gold, 452–459. University of Minnesota Press.

Hanel, Rachael. 2017. "Joycestick." *Poets & Writers Magazine* 45 (4): 15–17.

Hill, Tom. 2020. "Four Reports on the OA Monograph: Review." *Learned Publishing* 33 (3): 345–347. doi:10.1002/leap.1311

Kim, Dorothy. 2014. "Social Media and Academic Surveillance: The Ethics of Digital Bodies." *Model View Culture*, 2014. https://modelviewculture.com/pieces/social-media-and-academic-surveillance-the-ethics-of-digital-bodies

Lanier, Jaron. 2014. *Who Owns The Future?* London: Penguin.

Murphy, Órla, and Patrick Egan. 2023. "Sharing as CARE and FAIR in the Digital Humanities." In *The Bloomsbury Handbook to the Digital Humanities*, edited by James O'Sullivan, 267–271. London: Bloomsbury Academic. https://hdl.handle.net/10468/14776

Nyhan, Julianne, and Oliver Duke-Williams. 2014. "Joint and Multi-Authored Publication Patterns in the Digital Humanities." *Literary and Linguistic Computing* 29 (3): 387–399. doi:10.1093/llc/fqu018

O'Sullivan, James, Christopher P. Long, and Mark Mattson. 2016. "Dissemination as Cultivation: Scholarly Communications in a Digital Age." In *Doing Digital Humanities: Practice, Training, Research*, edited by Constance Crompton, Richard J. Lane, and Ray Siemens, 384–397. New York: Routledge.

Penier, Izabella, Martin Paul Eve, and Tom Grady. 2020. "Revenue Models for Open Access Monographs 2020." Community-led Open Publication Infrastructures for Monographs (COPIM). doi:10.5281/zenodo.4011836

Pressman, Jessica. 2020. *Bookishness: Loving Books in a Digital Age*. Columbia University Press.

Risam, Roopika. 2014. "Rethinking Peer Review in the Age of Digital Humanities." *Ada: A Journal of Gender, New Media, and Technology* 4. https://digitalcommons.salemstate.edu/english_facpub/3

Sample, Mark. 2013. "The Digital Humanities Is Not about Building, It's about Sharing." In *Defining Digital Humanities: A Reader*, edited by Melissa Terras, Julianne Nyhan, and Edward Vanhoutte, 255–257. Ashgate.

Suber, Peter. 2005. "Promoting Open Access in the Humanities." https://dash.harvard.edu/handle/1/4729720

Suber, Peter. 2012. *Open Access*. The MIT Press.

Suber, Peter. 2013. "Peter Suber on the State of Open Access: Where Are We, What Still Needs to Be Done?" Interview by Richard Poynder. http://poynder.blogspot.com/2013/07/peter-suber-on-state-of-open-access.html

Suber, Peter. 2017. "Why Is Open Access Moving So Slowly In The Humanities?" Blog of the APA (blog). https://blog.apaonline.org/2017/06/08/open-access-in-the-humanities-part-2/

Terras, Melissa. 2012. "The Impact of Social Media on the Dissemination of Research: Results of an Experiment." *Journal of Digital Humanities* 1 (3). http://journalofdigitalhumanities.org/1-3/the-impact-of-social-media-on-the-dissemination-of-research-by-melissa-terras/

Terras, Melissa. 2016. "Crowdsourcing in the Digital Humanities." In *A New Companion to Digital Humanities*, edited by Susan Schreibman, Ray Siemens, and John Unsworth, 420–439. Wiley-Blackwell.

Thompson, John B. 2012. *Merchants of Culture: The Publishing Business in the Twenty-First Century*, 2nd edn. Polity.

Underwood, Ted, David Bamman, and Sabrina Lee. 2018. "The Transformation of Gender in English-Language Fiction." *Journal of Cultural Analytics*. doi:10.22148/16.019

Wilkinson, Mark D., Michel Dumontier, Jan Aalbersberg, Gabrielle Appleton, Myles Axton, Arie Baak, Niklas Blomberg, et al. 2016. "The FAIR Guiding Principles for Scientific Data Management and Stewardship." *Scientific Data* 3 (March): 160018. doi:10.1038/sdata.2016.18

6

THE DARK SIDE OF DH

There once was a keynote, delivered in a lecture theatre at a prestigious ivy league university. The speaker delivered a measured and well-reasoned criticism of the digital humanities for the field's lack of diversity and inclusivity. They focused on race, gender, and inequality. The lecture, which was delivered with conviction and, undoubtedly, the best of intentions, was a strange experience given the context: the speaker was white, as was the *entirety* of their audience, and the venue was a private research university built on the ideals of elitism and marginalisation. If this keynote was intended as a rallying call to the community to do better, it was poorly set. The glaring absence of the underprivileged groups that this lecture sought to champion is ironic, but such absence is also evidence of need for such examinations of DH. This scene crystallises a central paradox of the digital humanities: critical commitments to equity and inclusion often sit uneasily alongside institutional practices that replicate hierarchy, exclusion, and unequal distributions of recognition and resources. The emergence of the digital humanities has brought much to our understanding of humanity and culture, but the field has not been immune from, and in some cases, has arguably heightened, the social disparities of our time.

DOI: 10.4324/9781351203395-6

DH, despite its progressive rhetoric, perpetuates harmful power structures through three interconnected mechanisms. Certain DH methodologies, particularly statistical criticism, embed masculinist and individualistic values that marginalise alternative ways of knowing. The field's material practices, from labour relations to conference cultures, systematically exclude already vulnerable communities. And DH's alignment with neoliberal logics transforms humanistic inquiry into a tool of economic instrumentalism. These represent the failure of DH to interrogate its own complicity in systems of domination. Meaningful progress requires acknowledgment of these problems, as well as fundamental restructuring of how we conceive and practice digital humanities.

If responses to criticisms of the DH community are anything to go by, any negative appraisal of the field will be met with severe resistance on public forums.[1] It is natural for scholars to leap to the defence of their discipline, but there have been occasions when resistance is a little too vociferous. Of course, the same charge could be levelled at some of the critiques, which often hide legitimate concerns in overwrought language—for example, characterising digital humanities as a wholesale instrument of neoliberal capture or as inherently antithetical to progressive scholarship. For the digital humanities to realise their potential, everyone needs to take a breath when offering and receiving criticism of the field. There is a lot about DH that is good, and there is a lot about DH that is bad. Much of this book has focused on the good, and so this chapter will present some of the bad.

When scholars speak of "the dark side of the digital humanities" (Grusin 2014; Smithies 2023), they are referring to the social, economic, and theoretical divides which exist in this space. When such perspectives emerge, the scholarly community at large needs to be better at how they are handled. When the reaction is a mass tirade on social media, nobody benefits, and the argument becomes about the meta-legitimacy of DH itself, as opposed to any specific issue or failing. This defensive response is itself symptomatic of the problem: a field so invested in its own progressive self-image that it cannot tolerate systematic critique.

And there are major failings within the digital humanities, some of which are symptoms of systemic inequalities that persist right across society, some of which are consequences of, or certainly have been exacerbated by, the presence of the digital. It is probably naïve idealism to think that we might ever eradicate these failings from the discipline, but certainly, by recognising such deficiencies, or simply by listening when others speak of faults that they perceive, we might at least make the digital humanities a little better, a little more humane.

STATISTICAL CRITICISM AS INDIVIDUALISTIC AND MASCULINIST

The critique of statistical criticism reveals how methodological choices in DH are never neutral but carry implicit values about legitimate knowledge production. Understanding this requires examining both the practice itself and the gendered dynamics it perpetuates.

Nan Z. Da's "The Computational Case against Computational Literary Studies" argues that the problem with digital methods is that there is "a fundamental mismatch between the statistical tools that are used and the objects to which they are applied" (Da 2019, 601). The efficacy of computer-assisted criticism has been defended throughout this book; of greater concern at this point is Katherine Bode's response to Da, posted on the *Critical Inquiry*-affiliated blog, *In the Moment* (Bode 2019).

Bode uses the opportunity to express several concerns with the very idea of what she calls "statistical criticism," problematising the centrality of computer-assisted literary criticism to DH. Her critique goes beyond methodological concerns to expose how this approach reinforces existing academic hierarchies. Bode draws comparisons between digital literary studies and other fields in the humanities, such as digital history, wherein the emphasis is on the construction of rich datasets. Bode cites *The Proceedings of the Old Bailey*, hosted by the University of Sheffield's Digital Humanities Institute, as one example of such a dataset. This resource appeals to Bode because it can be used by a wide range of researchers, and is suited to both computational and, most importantly, non-computational modes of analysis. Computational literary studies, on the other hand, is all about epistemological novelty, about individuals finding patterns which they alone utilise as the basis of publication. Bode asks: "Why is literary studies so hung up on (whether in favour of, or opposed to) this individualistic mode of statistical criticism?"

There is some merit to Bode's suggestion that statistical criticism is individualistic. Certainly, compared with larger digitisation and resource-building projects like *The Proceedings of the Old Bailey*, statistical criticism tends to lead to publications by one or a small team of individuals. The findings in such outputs are often presented, as Bode also reminds us (Bode 2017), without the relevant dataset, preventing others from replicating, disproving, or advancing upon the act of criticism. This practice of withholding data exemplifies what feminist scholars have long critiqued as a masculinist mode of knowledge production: competitive, proprietary, and focused on individual achievement rather than collective understanding. There are ways in which large digital resources are also individualistic, particularly when it comes to invisible labour, as it is often one or a few high-profile academics who are credited with "owning" such projects. However, as far as utility is concerned, Bode has a point. This is not to say that the significance of those findings produced through statistical criticism is diminished, but rather, by presenting such findings without an accompanying dataset, researchers retain control over that knowledge: they keep an essential part of that knowledge and how it was produced for themselves, and that is individualistic.[2]

Statistical criticism promises to disrupt the status quo by bringing us beyond the established canon and by allowing us to "look at *all* of literary history: canonical and noncanonical: together" (Moretti 2013). It would be unfair to suggest that we have not, in some respects, started down that path, but for every critical assumption that has been queried using statistics, some other element of the status quo has been reified, particularly the influence of privilege in the production of meaning. The promise of democratisation through data obscures how access to computational resources, technical training, and time for experimentation remain concentrated among the already privileged. As Bode writes, statistical criticism is dependent on resources which "privilege dominant literatures and literary cultures" (Bode 2019). Statistical methods do not in themselves unsettle the canon; any meaningful shift depends on the scope and diversity of the datasets to which those methods are applied. Digital methods will never disrupt existing hierarchies or cultural echelons if they operate on privileged materials, produced using privileged resources, published in return for individual prestige and professional capital.

Bode's assertion that statistical criticism "inhibit[s] the development of new, large-scale, collaborative environments for both computational and noncomputational literary research" is perhaps overstated (Bode 2019), in that it is typically far more expensive to produce large, digital resources like *The Proceedings of the Old Bailey*. The fact is that many institutions do not have the expertise or resources to produce such a project, and many countries do not have national funding agencies that could afford to fund such an endeavour, while many scholars work at institutions where individualistic research is precisely what will get them much-needed advancement. Nonetheless, it is positive to see that scholars invested in distant reading are now committing to initiatives designed to produce rich, multicultural datasets,[3] and thus start to "bridge the scholarly and critical—the curatorial and statistical—dimensions of (digital) literary studies" (Bode 2019). The tension between individual and collaborative work reflects deeper structural issues in academia that DH has failed to address.

In defence of the individual, were it not for individualistic acts of statistical criticism, the digital humanities might not have produced far more, but far less. Allowing DH to become something that can only be practised at large institutions or by large collaborations is equally perilous. Not only would this inevitably lead to further exclusion, part of what makes the humanities great is the potential for *individuals* to do great things. Lone scholars in their silos should be seen as caricatures, as symbols of some old, bleak world. Lone scholars in their silos have given us *so much*, and they will continue to do so. Computer-assisted criticism can be done by ill-equipped individuals, producing an awful lot of knowledge of very little investment, and once the knowledge is published, it is permanent, and its legacy is lasting. Da makes a similar point, asking "why we need 'labs' or the exorbitant funding that [computational literary studies] has garnered" (Da 2019, 603).

But the issue is a complex one, and while a lot can be achieved by the lone scholar with their laptop, financial privilege makes things a lot easier, providing access to superior hardware, proprietary systems and software, datasets, and support services. This creates a paradox: statistical criticism is simultaneously more accessible than large-scale projects and yet still excludes those without institutional resources. But the main reason that DH costs money, in answer to Da's question, is labour: the most expensive part of doing or teaching computer-assisted criticism is gaining access to the required expertise. Lone scholars can give us much, but if DH is to also have an alternative to the individual scholar who works alone in their office, investment in personnel is needed. Labs are just meeting places, but what matters is *who* one finds in the lab, what can be achieved not just in research but in classrooms, and there is nothing exorbitant about paying people tasked with supporting interdisciplinary work. The cost of DH labs, measured against other departments and faculties, is not excessive: it draws more attention these days because it generates new costs where the humanities used to be cheap.

Bode also accuses statistical criticism of being masculinist. Anecdotal evidence for this claim can be found in Chapter 2, wherein many of the studies which use text analysis to examine the language of gender have been written by men (Hoover 2013; Rybicki 2016; Weidman and O'Sullivan 2018). Furthermore, examining gender through the lens of cultural analytics can, as Laura Mandell argues, "produce clichés" or "stereotyping" (Mandell 2019). The problem is not just who conducts this research but how it conceptualises its object of study. It does so by "rewriting gender as sex," and while sex might provide statistical signals, conflating these two things for the purposes of constructing systems of classification is quantitatively and culturally problematic. The obsession of (mostly male) critics with computer-assisted analyses of male and female authorship tells us nothing of the language of gender, and yet, bold claims are being made based on statistical separations of sex. Mandell asks, why?

> First, why collect data according to the categories M/F? Capturing data as M/F will create statistically significant differences between M/F, but are they significant? And more importantly, what exactly do they signify?
>
> (Mandell 2019)

Mandell's questions expose how statistical criticism often reproduces rather than interrogates binary thinking about gender. When we use computational methods to "prove" differences between male and female writing, we risk essentialising gender differences that are socially constructed and historically contingent. Where similar questions have been posed by male critics using data-mining techniques to analyse literature, that same conflation of gender and sex is sometimes still present. There is something inherently masculinist in this field's need to constantly demonstrate the ability to separate male and female authors, even when efforts to do so are accompanied by an acknowledgment that doing so "transposes dangerous social oppositions with statistically-valid results" (O'Sullivan 2017). If one recognises this methodological limitation, why progress with the project in question? The answer reveals an uncomfortable truth: the demonstration of technical mastery often takes precedence over ethical considerations.

And yet, there remains something disconcerting in Bode's description of statistical criticism as masculinist. Certainly, there are examples of studies which use cultural analytics which might be construed as masculinist, but to state that statistical criticism is, in itself, a masculinist mode, effaces the many female experts and feminist scholars who do this kind of work, those who use cultural analytics, to quote Lisa Marie Rhody, for acts of "re-visioning":

> I dig because I believe that feminist literary studies can offer a necessary corrective to the androcentric tendencies of "big data," one that, in its unsettling, directly addresses the technological and epistemological challenges of our age.
>
> (Rhody 2016)

Rhody's perspective suggests that the problem lies not in the methods themselves but in how they are deployed and by whom. This raises crucial questions about whether DH can develop truly feminist approaches to computational analysis. It is clear from general observation that this branch of the digital humanities has a lot of men, perhaps disproportionately so, but that reflects the community, not the methods. If statistical criticism is perceived as masculinist, then that is a failing of DH. It is disappointing to see that our discipline has replicated gender disparities long documented in the sciences and engineering, not because such biases are intrinsic to computational tools, but because the training pathways, professional cultures, and institutional reward structures that accompany those tools often reproduce existing inequalities.

DIVERSITY, INCLUSIVITY AND THE DIGITAL HUMANITIES

The gendered dynamics of statistical criticism are symptomatic of broader failures of diversity and inclusion in DH. These failures manifest themselves not just in who participates but in whose knowledge is valued and how power operates within the field.

Writing for the 2019 incarnation of *Debates in the Digital Humanities*, Safiya Umoja Noble, Co-Founder and Co-Director of the UCLA Center for Critical Internet Inquiry and author of the hugely influential text, *Algorithms of Oppression* (2018), starts her essay with reference to a room full of white people. Noble cites Audre Lorde's 1984 conference speech "The Master's Tools Will Never Dismantle the Master's House," which she explains, "was addressed to an audience of white feminists largely unconcerned with the many missing intellectual contributions of Black women to the fields of feminist theory and practice" (Noble 2019). Noble believes that there is much the digital humanities can learn from Lorde's lecture, specifically, how our reliance on digital tools and technologies reinforces existing structures of power:

> Lorde's speech was part of a Black radical feminist tradition, which, among other critical Black intellectual movements, we might welcome into the field of digital humanities. These movements allow us to see

> how, rather than making Black life and the lives of other people of color solely the subjects of archival and preservation practice, we might also consider the degree to which our very reliance on digital tools, of the master or otherwise, exacerbates existing patterns of exploitation and at times even creates new ones.
>
> (Noble 2019)

Noble's invocation of Lorde crystallises a fundamental challenge: can tools developed within systems of oppression ever be truly liberatory? This question becomes more urgent when we examine how DH operates in practice. Social critics have long represented technology as that which sustains the status quo. Theodor W. Adorno and Max Horkheimer, two of the twentieth century's most prominent philosophers, often portray science and technology as the propellent of capitalist ideology (Adorno and Horkheimer 2002). Their critique gains new relevance in the digital age, where algorithms and platforms don't just reflect but actively shape social hierarchies.

That is not to say that invention is inherently bad, but one need only look at Google and Facebook to see how technology can drive extreme concentrations of wealth and power. The humanities have long harboured the intellectual and critical cohorts necessary to resist such concentration, but the digital humanities have detracted from that mission. DH can often serve as a distraction, in that we have "become overly invested in the digital to the exclusion of pressing social issues of racial injustice, disenfranchisement, and community transformation" (Noble 2019). And while many digital projects claim to liberate and preserve marginalised cultures, the methods and techniques of the digital humanities are, to quote Roopika Risam, the architects of the emerging field of Postcolonial DH, "built on the histories and traditions of humanities knowledge production that have been deeply implicated in both colonialism and neocolonialism" (Risam 2018a, 4). As Noble puts it, "the technological engagements they rest on are not free from political consequence" (Noble 2019). These political consequences become visible when we examine who participates in DH and under what conditions.

Foremost among these consequences is the lack of diversity and inclusivity to be found in the digital humanities.[4] The digital humanities are very white (McPherson 2012). The digital humanities are often dominated by men (Bailey 2011). The digital humanities rely on forms of labour and service which reinforce problematic social hierarchies (Brown 2018). The digital humanities can efface matters of difference and identity, like queerness (Ruberg et al. 2018; Boyd and Ruberg 2023). The digital humanities exploit and reduce individuals to data points, and data points are never neutral (Earhart 2018). The digital humanities undermine the human subject (Risam 2018b). The digital humanities promote western over global perspectives (Aiyegbusi 2018). The digital humanities have a class problem, wherein access to datasets and techniques can be dictated solely by the means of institutions and individuals (Prescott 2016; O'Sullivan 2023). The digital humanities rely on forms of labour which are often precarious, underappreciated, or completely unrecognised (Boyles et al. 2018; Ross and Pilsch 2019). The digital humanities undoubtedly have many other problems, but these issues of diversity and inclusion are among the most pressing. DH has a representation problem (Eichmann-Kalwara et al. 2019), the remedying of which will take a concerted, collective effort. Central to this representation problem is the issue of invisible labour, which deserves detailed examination.

A major part of that effort needs to be the eradication of the invisible labour on which endeavours in the digital humanities are often built. DH scholars often champion collaboration as one of the ways in which the digital humanities improve upon their traditional counterparts, but the chief danger and a frequent reality of collaboration is that individuals get credit for work that they have not done and skills they do not possess. This is not merely an issue of fairness but of how knowledge production is structured in ways that systematically devalue certain forms of expertise. Collaboration is a wonderful ideal, but the culture of academia, certainly the culture of the humanities, is such that one figure is often cast as the central intellectual stakeholder in any project, and they take much of the glory. Even with massive, grant-funded initiatives, there is often a principal investigator or project leader to whom ownership of the work is often assigned. Projects and collaborations need leaders, and these leaders are often the people who developed the idea, but the outputs of such undertakings produce professional capital that is being exchanged for promotions and security that is not equally shared across all contributors, even though the work could not have been done by any one individual. Why is it that the high-profile scholars who lead large interdisciplinary projects are entitled to exchange the accomplishments of that collaboration for economic betterment, but many of their co-workers, particularly those who provide what might be categorised as "support services," usually get nothing? The answer lies in how academic hierarchies value different forms of labour. "Intellectual" work is privileged over "technical" work, even when the technical work requires sophisticated expertise and creative problem-solving (i.e. intellectual work). This hierarchy is deeply reliant on class differences.

There are countless examples of DH projects where the principal investigator would not be able to reproduce the methodology or resource framework without support from colleagues in services like IT, and yet, it is their name that is known and it is their job that is protected and it is their salary that increases. There is so much labour in the digital humanities that goes unacknowledged in the real, material sense of acknowledgment. This is possibly because interdisciplinarity and collaboration are still relatively new in the humanities, and we do not yet have disciplinary cultures or institutional models suited to appreciating everyone who contributes to the production of knowledge. It is possible that, in the desperate struggle for survival, many scholars do not care about an equal distribution of professional capital, and have accepted that they will need to exploit the expertise of others to produce the work that they need for their own progression. This dynamic is hardly unique to DH and is endemic across contemporary academia, but because DH relies so heavily on collaborative and technical labour, the asymmetries of credit and reward become more acute and more visible.

As discussed in Chapter 1, Matthew Kirschenbaum has thoroughly explored this problematic use of DH as a "tactical" term, "unabashedly deployed" (Kirschenbaum 2012a) by scholars and academic professionals of all ranks and type seeking to appear professionally more attractive in an "increasingly monstrous institutional terrain" (Kirschenbaum 2012b). Some of these tacticians possibly deserve sympathy, and are not all charlatans (Unsworth 2002), but are genuine, talented scholars who are fighting a battle with precarity that most will lose. This sympathy, however, should not obscure how tactical uses of DH perpetuate exclusion. While useful as an epistemic provocation in the exploration of the discipline, there is some generosity in taking it easy on the "who's in and who's out" conversation. The discourse that surrounds such debates can sometimes be unreasonably exclusionary, and it almost always ignores the realities of those individuals who have been forced into the shady opportunism that DH presents. The digital humanities would not have a charlatan problem if higher education was not built on precarious labour. DH will remain "tactical" as long as the terrain remains "monstrous," and for every Busa and Watson, for every full professor who led a DH project, there will be dozens of workers whose labour goes unrecognised and unrewarded (Nyhan and Terras 2017). This dynamic is exacerbated by what might be called DH's "celebrity culture," a phenomenon not unique to this field and common in emerging disciplines, but arguably intensified here by the centrality of digital visibility and social media to professional identity within DH.

Part of the problem is that the digital humanities have a celebrity problem, wherein the community, more highly attuned to the dynamics of social media than other disciplines, often confuses visibility for accomplishment. Many of the field's "famous" scholars have built their profiles by simply talking about digital humanities on platforms like Twitter/X, becoming known through activities like "live-tweeting" conferences, rather than producing proper, long-form critical arguments or novel interpretations. This creates a feedback loop where those with the time and cultural capital to maintain an online presence gain influence, while those doing the actual work of building and maintaining DH infrastructure remain invisible. Engaging in those activities that allow one to develop an international profile that is based on visibility rather than scholarship requires privilege of all sorts, both economic and cultural. For example, if one is to win the Busa or Zampolli prize, the two major awards for accomplishment in the field of DH, it would seem that being seen by western DH communities is the major requirement. These are supposedly international prizes, but the list of recipients would suggest that contributions to North American or the larger European DH communities are a prerequisite for winning.

There are scholars doing important work in the digital humanities who are not on Twitter, and there are DH communities which exist beyond the powerhouses of North America and central Europe. The assumption that "real" DH happens in English-speaking, Western contexts perpetuates a form of digital colonialism that the field claims to oppose. Of course, there are many wonderful scholars in these places, and distinguishing between scholarly cultures based on geographic and political constructs like nation can be deeply problematic because it usually leads to misplaced assumptions. We need to trust that scholars are doing the work that they feel needs to be done, prioritising and treating materials that are important to *their* own local culture, however they themselves have configured that culture. Furthermore, cross-cultural initiatives, even when appropriate, can be difficult to achieve (Mahony 2018), and require resources often beyond the reach of smaller institutions and national funding agencies.

But as far as international bodies, gatherings, and initiatives are concerned, members of the DH community need to remember that *their* world is not *the* world. Sometimes, we could all be a degree better off at just staying silent, at leaving space for those marginalised scholars and communities within our discipline to have a voice. Bowing out of the conversation, rather than continuing to monopolise it for one's own perspective, is often the most inclusive act. Such silence might allow for the emergence of unseen groups and fledgling communities of practice, and for the publication and consumption of more national and culture-specific archaeologies, produced by scholars working in those very same cultures and national contexts. But even well-intentioned calls for inclusion can reproduce exclusionary dynamics.

Believing in the possibility of "a public sphere in which no one was excluded" is presented by Anne Burdick, Johanna Drucker,

Peter Lunenfeld, Todd Presner, and Jeffrey Schnapp as "a core human value of the Digital Humanities" (Burdick et al. 2012). They acknowledge that a digital world where participation is "possible for everyone, anywhere, anytime" is something of a utopian ideal, but that believing in such ideals is at least something. But whose utopia is this? The vision of universal digital participation assumes access to electricity, devices, literacy, and time, resources that remain unequally distributed globally. More troublingly, it assumes that everyone wants to participate in digital culture on terms set by Western institutions. A future that allows for "participation without condition" would fix so much that is wrong with our society, but sceptics would be justifiably wary of such a world, a world which would have to be digital. Such a world might see the local priorities of smaller, emerging communities co-opted by imperious mores and institutions, while an even greater measure of our lives and intellectual endeavours is drawn into platforms developed by a select few companies, based in a select few countries, governed by a select few rules and regulations. Such a space might be wonderfully participatory, but it would not be conducive to good scholarship, and all that it entails in this age.

DH AS NEOLIBERAL LOGIC

Exclusions and hierarchies are not accidental but arise from DH's embeddedness within neoliberal structures. The field serves institutional and economic interests that often conflict with humanistic values. This future where we all do the same things, the same digital way using the same digital tools is one which we are racing towards willingly. In education, much of that homogenisation is being done under the DH umbrella. It is easy to see why so many institutions, starved of resources, have embraced the digital humanities without really considering what DH really is, or more importantly, how it should be configured locally in order to enrich their own communities and improve the lives of their own students. But in a world where the humanities are being increasingly devalued by students, parents, policymakers, and funding bodies, scope for such reflection is a luxury that many administrators simply cannot afford. DH becomes attractive precisely because it promises to make the humanities "relevant" in market terms: a promise that fundamentally misunderstands both the humanities and the market. The digital humanities have become a means through which the humanities might be "saved," made "more relevant" in the eyes of publics which have completely lost sight of the value of programmes in the arts and humanities.

And so, as has been noted various times throughout this book, the present moment is one in which DH is often hijacked by scholars, administrators, and institutions looking to survive this neoliberal world of ours. Richard Grusin gives us a suitable summary of the situation:

> Put most starkly, academics on the left blame the crisis in the humanities on the corporatization of the academy and the neoliberal insistence that the value of higher education is chiefly economic. Conversely, it is precisely because of the apparently instrumental or utilitarian value of the digital humanities that university administrators, foundation officers, and government agencies are so eager to fund DH projects, create DH undergraduate and graduate programs, and hire DH faculty.
>
> (Grusin 2014)

This instrumental value is not inherent to digital methods but arises from how they are framed and deployed within institutional contexts. The more that DH is commandeered by those who are solely interested in such instrumentality, the more it will be seen as part of the neoliberal logic which is currently decimating higher education. Administrators will continue to dissolve and amalgamate departments in long-established disciplines, while simultaneously founding new centres and creating new jobs in the digital humanities, and more scholars and practitioners will need to sacrifice their would-be commitment to other disciplines in the hope of finding stable employment. Understandably frustrated, even angry, with the sustained lack of institutional and public support for their respective fields, scholars in the wider humanities will point the finger at DH for appropriating resources that once belonged to others. DH scholars and initiatives, benefitting from some favour in a domain where there is very little favour to go around, will progress as though this is all just natural selection, sowing further discord, and reifying the metric-driven thinking that first brought us to this contentious pass.

Daniel Allington, Sarah Brouillette, and David Golumbia address such matters in an essay published in the *Los Angeles Review of Books*, arguing that the digital humanities are playing a major role in "the displacement of politically progressive humanities scholarship and activism" (Allington et al. 2016). Their critique deserves careful attention, not dismissal, as it exposes uncomfortable truths about DH's institutional function. They essentially argue that DH is serving the corporatisation of education by turning scholars and graduates of the humanities into something that appeals to the interests of capitalist enterprise: "Neoliberal policies and institutions value academic work that produces findings immediately usable by industry and that produces graduates trained for the current requirements of the commercial workplace." DH, according to this now notorious essay,[5] only serves to consolidate existing structures of power, replacing the traditional values of the arts and humanities with more utilitarian material that is easier to sell to various governing and industry bodies, policymakers, fee-paying students and their parents. The digital humanities are really about promoting "technical expertise as a form (indeed, the superior form) of humanist knowledge," they are about employing "Silicon Valley buzzwords that cast other approaches in a remarkably negative light," and they are about major research institutions consolidating "their grip on available research funding," creating market dominance in the manner of conglomerates like Facebook and Google. And in doing these things, DH will stealthily erode those fields that university management see as outmoded and financially unprofitable. While this critique may seem overstated, it identifies real tensions in how DH positions itself institutionally.

Allington, Brouillette, and Golumbia (2016) accept that the digital humanities may be "unintentionally" facilitating the neoliberalisation of education, a noteworthy concession on their part because this seems to be the prevailing narrative across both the field's proponents and detractors. And one can see why this narrative suits both sides. If a paucity of institutional resources and a lack of public and political support for the humanities are to blame for scholars and their administrators being forced to adopt the digital in a desperate attempt to stay relevant, those practising DH can be blamed for their complicity, introducing and developing a disciplinary culture which gives those in power the excuse they are looking for to dismantle those existing programs, departments, and methodologies. But this narrative can also be used to absolve DH practitioners of their guilt; in a world where all disciplines were treated equally, the digital humanities would no longer promote the neoliberal agenda, leaving the field and its acolytes alone to do their work, to grow organically without concern for charlatans and tacticians.

Deliberating between these two camps would only distract from the matter at hand, and certainly, it is easy to sympathise with both views. There is also some naïvety, and a bit of privilege, in each attitude. The truth is more complex: DH both resists and reproduces neoliberal logics, often simultaneously. Overhyping the extent to which DH contributes to the ongoing neoliberalisation of higher education betrays something of a wistfulness for a truly public academia that really never was, or certainly, has not been for a very long time. Equally, in downplaying all of this, DH scholars allow the civic value and integrity of their discipline to be eroded in exchange for personal security. The digital humanities, like any discipline, cannot exist outside of late capitalism, but that does not mean its advocates should give up on resisting the metrification and privatisation of their professions and institutions. And even if it were possible for scholars and their departments to build such an ideological utopia, the students and graduates of higher education, like many of the DH charlatans, still need to survive in the real world, the neoliberal world. As uncomfortable as it might be for educators to admit, students cannot simply be taught to recognise the social dynamics of the world we live in, they must also be taught to survive in a market that is designed to be hostile to society-at-large. Only very privileged teachers and learners can show disregard for that reality, whereas everyone else needs to worry about how best to sell their labour, how to produce evidence in popular forms, and how to find opportunity in those few remaining industries that enjoy the support of politicians and wealthy privateers (O'Sullivan 2023). The challenge is not to choose between complicity and resistance but to understand how DH operates within these constraints while seeking spaces for critical intervention.

There is truth and there is naïvety in both of these perspectives, and so one should be allowed to say, without condemnation and remaining an advocate for its development, that DH is, in part, born of neoliberal logic. The most significant difference between digital humanities and other disciplines within the humanities is the particular ways in which the former uses computers, and computer systems to replicate, maintain, and further the structures of imperial capitalism. This is not a superficial connection but fundamental to how digital systems operate. In an interview for the *Los Angeles Review of Books* that preceded his infamous essay, Golumbia argues that DH is making English a "much more quiescent field." He says:

> Database analysis on the history of literature has replaced encouraging students to defuse their deepest political hatreds. That kind of political focus seems to have gone away. There was optimism in English before DH came along and the optimism was not a Silicon Valley vision of computers solving the world's problems.
>
> (Golumbia 2016)

Golumbia's characterisation may be reductive, but it points to a real shift in how literary studies conceives its social function. And of course, whenever Silicon Valley attempts to solve a problem, it is usually because there is profit to be made, or someone who has already made their fortune is afflicted by it. Buzzwords like "innovation," "creativity," "disruption" are used like the old "Uncle Sam Wants You" posters designed to recruit soldiers during World War I and World War II. Answering such calls means that any genuine newness that might be achieved is done so on the part of those few tech giants which control the world's digital technologies, and so rather than achieving something other, that invention only serves to strengthen existing conditions.

The digital humanities must admit that many of those ideologies we hold dear, such as open access, are not always as progressive as the discourse surrounding them would have us believe. This is particularly evident when we examine how open access intersects with platform capitalism. As discussed in Chapter 5, giving content and information away freely allows tech firms to make huge profits from data that has been acquired without cost (Lanier 2014). As long as individuals and institutions continue to give personal and cultural data to tech giants, without any form of material compensation or control, the power of these organisations, both in terms of capital and influence, will only grow. The more we give these organisations, the more they are positioned to sell to us, to manipulate us and direct our behaviours (Zuboff 2019). DH, by making screens an inherent part of the humanities, has transformed what was once a site of resistance into a new pool from which Silicon Valley can recruit.[6] The implications extend beyond individual platforms to the entire infrastructure of digital knowledge production.

Imperialism once had geography to consider, but the digital means that the forces of late capitalism no longer need to contend with frontiers. Social dynamics and cultural conversations across the world are increasingly mediated through platforms and services produced in specific cultural contexts, usually American. It is not overly dramatic to state that Silicon Valley dictates how we find and consume information, how we work, how we interact, and how we occupy ourselves during leisure time. The structural inequality that made these organisations what they are is then reproduced through their platforms (O'Neil 2016). This can also be seen in the scholarly community, where smaller cultural contexts are dwarfed by the issues, activities, and idiosyncrasies of larger nations. And we remain, for the most part, uncritical of this turn because of the status that computers hold in contemporary culture (Golumbia 2009), in education, and alarmingly, the humanities in the digital age.

It is alarming because those of us in the humanities should know better, we should know that, for all we have achieved and might yet achieve with computers, it is quite reckless to allow these systems to redefine disciplines and practices without careful pause and consideration. We all think we have done such due diligence, but really, when we are honest with ourselves, the truth is that any reflection we have done has been insufficient, because we have failed. This failure manifests itself in multiple ways that demand enumeration. That is not to say that we should abandon the DH project to halt the spread of neoliberalism in the humanities, but if we could just own the failings of our discipline, we might lessen their impact, if even a little.

Administrators are reconfiguring departments, hires, and pedagogical offerings based on metrics like student numbers, grant income, and the promise of technology to improve them. This is neoliberal logic. Research and teaching that advocates for the use of computer-assisted literary and cultural analytics promotes metric-driven sensibilities, suggesting that nothing can be known unless it can be quantified. This is neoliberal logic. One of the major instruments of capitalism is the allure of convenience, the promise of an easier, more elegant fix. In some of the best-loved tools of DH, understanding has been utterly supplanted by black-box functions that produce quick and easy results that can be exchanged, through publication, for professional, and then possibly economic, capital. Convenience is commodified through DH summer schools and workshops which sell the promise of expertise and community to those who can pay. Mass digitisation ignores the concerns of those who wish to remain outside the digital, eradicating the personal and cultural privacies and rights of individual and communities. Money, labour, and carbon are wasted in the creation of unsustainable resources that have a direct ecological impact. Unsustainable projects are pursued as scholars and universities seek to satisfy personal and institutional interests and vanity, and build empires: "The cumulative effects of mass-scale digital infrastructures, products, and engagements require a debt of energy and resources that we cannot collectively repay to the earth or to humanity" (Noble 2019). Recognising these patterns as elements in the structure of neoliberal logic is the first step toward developing alternatives. But such recognition must also acknowledge how DH's alignment with scientific methods furthers these neoliberal transformations.

THE SCIENTIFICATION OF THE HUMANITIES

The neoliberal transformation of the humanities through DH is inseparable from what might be called the scientification of humanistic inquiry, the increasing dominance of quantitative methods and scientific epistemologies in fields traditionally defined by interpretive and critical approaches. The "this is just the world" retort is weak. The digital humanities cannot be immune from wider social, cultural, and economic failings, but that does not allow the community to carry on in ignorance while transgressions against the few seep into the community. The humanities and higher education suffered from issues of representation long before the digital, but the digital has made a lot of the bad stuff worse. As the humanities grow to be more a part of the sciences, the issues of representation and power ingrained within the latter will gradually seep into disciplines which traditionally have not hitherto suffered from them. This scientification operates through multiple mechanisms.

The type of analytical work that is considered by many in the community to be "real" DH is often done by men, because men are more likely to grow up in situations where they are encouraged to develop technical skills. And men, as Miriam Posner reminds us, are often more comfortable working in the environments that tend to emerge around male-dominated practices:

> First, men—middle-class white men, to be specific—are far more likely to have been given access to a computer and encouraged to use it at a young age. I love that you learned BASIC at age ten. But please realize that this has not been the case for all of us.
> Second, the "culture of code," the inside jokes and joshing that you enjoy, may not be equally appealing to everyone who encounters it. This should be, but apparently isn't, obvious.
>
> (Posner 2012)

Posner's observations point to how technical competence becomes a gatekeeping mechanism that reproduces existing hierarchies while claiming to democratise knowledge. And furthermore, as an increasing number of scholars turn to mastering scientific tools and methods, fewer will be left to do those non-digital forms of work once so central to the humanities. As Eileen Gardiner and Ronald G. Musto ask, "is the digital hurting the humanities by drawing scholars away from the traditional work of humanists and turning them into number crunchers or bell-and-whistle builders?" (Gardiner and Musto 2015, 5). This question becomes more urgent when we consider what is lost in this transformation.

Notwithstanding Stephen Ramsay's eloquent reflection on the value of building (Ramsay 2013, 243–45), a scholar of the humanities should be concerned with far more than the manufacture of tools and resources. The more we rely on technology for access and analysis, the more we risk distancing ourselves from the objects of culture, morphing from experts into passive users. This passivity is not merely technical but epistemological: we begin to accept that only what can be computed can be known. If we allow computer systems to become ever-present conduits between ourselves and our humanity, they will act on us with far more authority than we are positioned to act upon them. Eventually, as Heidegger warns us in *The Question Concerning Technology*—essential reading for any practitioner of DH—we will only ever be able to see the world instrumentally, in terms of resources that can feed some functional purpose (Heidegger 1977). When this is how we think, it becomes very difficult to answer the great questions of culture and humanity.

Joseph Weizenbaum, a pioneer of artificial intelligence, wrote about this troubling turn back in the late seventies:

> When I say that science has been gradually converted into a slow-acting poison, I mean that the attribution of certainty to scientific knowledge by the common wisdom, an attribution now made so nearly universally that it has become a commonsense dogma, has virtually delegitimatized all other ways of understanding.
>
> (Weizenbaum 1977, 16)

> The belief in the indispensability of the computer is not entirely mistaken. The computer becomes an indispensable component of any structure once it is so thoroughly integrated with the structure, so enmeshed in various vital substructures, that it can no longer be factored out without fatally impairing the whole structure.
>
> (Weizenbaum 1977, 28)

Weizenbaum's warnings have proven prescient. In DH, we see exactly this process: computational methods become so embedded in our practices that we forget they are tools, not truths. The digital humanities, and wider humanities, have much to learn from Weizenbaum. There is much value in interdisciplinarity, but if we continue to let scientific principles and agendas govern the formation of a new humanities where certain types of knowledge production are deemed compulsory, we will lose so much. We need to stop expecting and encouraging quantitative evidence in situations where critical interpretation arrived at through human intuition alone is sufficient. We need to stop assuming that there are outmoded disciplines and intellectual practices that desperately need the salvation promised by the digital. We need to remember, as Weizenbaum does, that there was a time when literature and the arts were seen for more than their aesthetic value, as more than entertainment, but as "vehicles for understanding the societies they represented" (Weizenbaum 1977, 16). Those who wish to merge such vehicles with the knowing afforded through computer-assisted methods should be allowed to do so, but those who wish to just read, to just close read in the long-established sense, should not be punished for creating meaning that is not considered "scientifically" valid. The pressure to be "scientific" reflects deeper anxieties about the value of humanities in a world that increasingly prizes only instrumental knowledge.

While everyone might disagree on the ideal constitution, the digital humanities should contain a lot of the humanities, and a little bit of the sciences. If it is the other way around, and scientific ways of seeing and knowing are privileged, what you have is something else, maybe still DH, but a very different kind that really cannot be said to exist as a form of humanities. If the digital humanities are, returning to Kathleen Fitzpatrick, the humanities, just done digitally (Fitzpatrick 2012), then they need to be just that and not the sciences, done digitally. It is possible that scholars and practitioners working in this field lose sight of that important distinction, or worse, forget how the tenets of DH threaten to gnaw at those disciplines which have resisted the instrumental promise of new technologies. This is not an argument against interdisciplinarity but for a more critical understanding of how disciplinary hierarchies operate when fields merge. The humanities have their own rigorous methods and epistemologies that should not be abandoned in the rush to appear "scientific."

Not everyone in the digital humanities has contributed to the issues presented throughout this chapter, but everyone in DH, if they are to see this field prosper, should take some responsibility for such failings. The digital humanities will always be imperfect, but we must have some faith in the possibility that we can reach a future where those current imperfections are at least diminished. That will take time, reflection, effort, discourse across local and international communities, and a willingness to engage in uncomfortable conversations. Nickoal Eichmann-Kalwara, Jeana Jorgensen, and Scott B. Weingart provided the perfect remarks on which to conclude this penultimate chapter: "The digital humanities will never be perfect. It embodies the worst of its criticisms and the best of its ideals, sometimes simultaneously" (Eichmann-Kalwara et al. 2019).

The so-called dark side of DH is central to understanding what the field is and might become. Methodological biases, systemic exclusions, neoliberal complicity, and epistemological narrowing are interconnected manifestations of how power operates through and within the digital humanities. Addressing them requires more than good intentions or incremental reforms. It demands fundamental questioning of our assumptions about what constitutes legitimate knowledge, whose voices matter, and what purposes our work serves. Only by confronting these dark sides directly can DH hope to realise its transformative potential without reproducing the very structures of domination it claims to challenge. DH, like any field, will never be perfect, but it can be honest about its imperfections and committed to doing better.

RECOMMENDED READING

Golumbia, David. 2009. *The Cultural Logic of Computation*. Cambridge, MA: Harvard University Press.

Lanier, Jaron. 2014. *Who Owns The Future?* London: Penguin.

Rooney, Ellen, and Elizabeth Weed, eds. 2014. "In the Shadows of the Digital Humanities." *Differences: A Journal of Feminist Cultural Studies*, 25 (1).

Smithies, James. 2023. "The Dark Side of DH." In *The Bloomsbury Handbook to the Digital Humanities*, edited by James O'Sullivan, 111–121. London: Bloomsbury Academic.

Zuboff, Shoshana. 2019. *The Age of Surveillance Capitalism: The Fight for a Human Future at the New Frontier of Power.* Profile Books.

NOTES

1 I once asked a peer to write a critique of DH for a project I was editing. They declined, offering the following explanation: "DH people are, frankly, a bit scary. They are very vocal online."

2 It is important to recognise that there are many instances where researchers cannot share the datasets, such as where copyright restrictions apply, but the realities of intellectual property law should not distract us from what is an important theoretical discussion.

3 See, for example, *Distant Reading for European Literary History* (COST Action CA16204): www.cost.eu/actions/CA16204/

4 As a straight, white, English-speaking man who has enjoyed a measure of upward social mobility because of stable, public-sector employment, I appreciate that I am possibly the worst person to write this section of this book. But I do hope that readers will conclude that I have treated these matters seriously, drawing upon and synthesising the work of scholars and thinkers whose perspectives come from a less privileged position than my own.

5 For whatever it is worth, I feel that the outrage that this essay generated on social media at the time of its publication was a little overzealous. At times, the style and tone of the essay does itself little favours, but it does present some arguments that we would all do well to reflect upon (ideally, in a calm and measured way). As far as "attacks" on DH are concerned, this essay really is worthwhile reading.

6 It is worth noting that there are imperial tendencies across all disciplines, as well as militant personalities who insist upon their specific cohort's agenda, and this is how it will always be because all students and scholars think their materials and methods are the most critical, the most noble. DH is not the first and will not be the last discipline—even within the humanities—to take a larger allocation of the resources than others think it deserves.

REFERENCES

Aiyegbusi, Babalola Titilola. 2018. "Decolonizing Digital Humanities: Africa in Perspective." In *Bodies of Information: Intersectional Feminism and the Digital Humanities*, edited by Elizabeth Losh and Jacqueline Wernimont, 434–446. University of Minnesota Press. doi:10.5749/j.ctv9hj9r9.26

Allington, Daniel, Sarah Brouillette, and David Golumbia. 2016. "Neoliberal Tools (and Archives): A Political History of Digital Humanities." *Los Angeles Review of Books*. https://lareviewofbooks.org/article/neoliberal-tools-archives-political-history-digital-humanities/#!

Bailey, Moya Z. 2011. "All the Digital Humanists Are White, All the Nerds Are Men, but Some of Us Are Brave." *Journal of Digital Humanities* 1 (1). http://journalofdigitalhumanities.org/1-1/all-the-digital-humanists-are-white-all-the-nerds-are-men-but-some-of-us-are-brave-by-moya-z-bailey/

Bode, Katherine. 2017. "The Equivalence of 'Close' and 'Distant' Reading; or, Toward a New Object for Data-Rich Literary History." *Modern Language Quarterly* 78 (1): 77–106. doi:10.1215/00267929-3699787

Bode, Katherine. 2019. "Computational Literary Studies: Participant Forum Responses, Day 2." In the Moment (blog). 2019. https://critinq.wordpress.com/2019/04/02/computational-literary-studies-participant-forum-responses-day-2-3/

Boyd, Jason, and Bo Ruberg. 2023. "Queer Digital Humanities." In *The Bloomsbury Handbook to the Digital Humanities*, edited by James O'Sullivan, 63–73. London: Bloomsbury Academic. doi:10.32920/23546031.v1

Boyles, Christina, Anne Cong-Huyen, Carrie Johnston, Jim McGrath, and Amanda Phillips. 2018. "Precarious Labor and the Digital Humanities." *American Quarterly* 70 (3): 693–700. doi:10.1353/aq.2018.0054

Brown, Susan. 2018. "Delivery Service: Gender and the Political Unconscious of Digital Humanities." In *Bodies of Information: Intersectional Feminism and the Digital Humanities*, edited by Elizabeth Losh and Jacqueline Wernimont, 261–286. University of Minnesota Press. doi:10.5749/j.ctv9hj9r9.18

Burdick, Anne, Johanna Drucker, Peter Lunenfeld, Todd Presner, and Jeffrey Schnapp. 2012. *Digital_Humanities*. Cambridge: The MIT Press.

Da, Nan Z. 2019. "The Computational Case against Computational Literary Studies." *Critical Inquiry* 45 (3): 601–639. doi:10.1086/702594

Earhart, Amy E. 2018. "Can We Trust the University?: Digital Humanities Collaborations with Historically Exploited Cultural Communities." In *Bodies of Information: Intersectional Feminism and the Digital Humanities*, edited by Elizabeth Losh and Jacqueline Wernimont, 369–390. University of Minnesota Press. doi:10.5749/j.ctv9hj9r9.23

Eichmann-Kalwara, Nickoal, Jeana Jorgensen, and Scott B. Weingart. 2019. "Representation at Digital Humanities Conferences (2000–2015)." In *Bodies of Information: Intersectional Feminism and the Digital Humanities*, edited by Elizabeth Losh and Jacqueline Wernimont, 72–92. University of Minnesota Press.

Fitzpatrick, Kathleen. 2012. "The Humanities, Done Digitally." In *Debates in the Digital Humanities*, edited by Matthew K. Gold. University of Minnesota Press. https://dhdebates.gc.cuny.edu/read/untitled-88c11800-9446-469ba3be-3fdb36bfbd1e/section/65e208fc-a5e6-479f-9a47-d51cd9c35e84

Gardiner, Eileen, and Ronald G. Musto. 2015. *The Digital Humanities: A Primer for Students and Scholars*. Cambridge University Press.

Golumbia, David. 2009. *The Cultural Logic of Computation*. Cambridge, MA: Harvard University Press.

Golumbia, David. 2016. "The Digital in the Humanities: An Interview with David Golumbia." Interview by Melissa Dinsman. *Los Angeles Review of Books*. https://lareviewofbooks.org/article/digital-humanities-interview-david-golumbia/

Grusin, Richard. 2014. "The Dark Side of Digital Humanities: Dispatches from Two Recent MLA Conventions." *Differences: A Journal of Feminist Cultural Studies* 25 (1): 79–92. doi:10.1215/10407391-2420009

Heidegger, Martin. 1977. "The Question Concerning Technology." In *The Question Concerning Technology and Other Essays*, translated by William Lovitt. New York: Harper Perennial.

Hoover, David L. 2013. "Textual Analysis." In *Literary Studies in the Digital Age*, edited by Kenneth M. Price and Ray Siemens. Modern Language Association of America. http://dlsanthology.commons.mla.org/textual-analysis/

Horkheimer, Max, and Theodor W. Adorno. 2002. *Dialectic of Enlightenment*. Edited by Gunzelin Noeri. Translated by Edmund Jephcott. Stanford University Press.

Kirschenbaum, Matthew. 2012a. "Digital Humanities As/Is a Tactical Term." In *Debates in the Digital Humanities*, edited by Matthew K. Gold. University of Minnesota Press. https://dhdebates.gc.cuny.edu/read/untitled-88c11800-9446-469b-a3be-3fdb36bfbd1e/section/cob0a8ee-95f0-4a9c-9451-e8ad168e3db5

Kirschenbaum, Matthew. 2012b. "What Is Digital Humanities and What's It Doing in English Departments?" In *Debates in the Digital Humanities*, edited by Matthew K. Gold. University of Minnesota Press. https://dhdebates.gc.cuny.edu/read/untitled-88c11800-9446-469b-3be-3fdb36bfbd1e/section/f5640d43-b8eb-4d49-bc4b-eb31a16f3d06

Lanier, Jaron. 2014. *Who Owns The Future?* London: Penguin.

Mahony, Simon. 2018. "Cultural Diversity and the Digital Humanities." *Fudan Journal of the Humanities and Social Sciences* 11 (3): 371–388. doi:10.1007/s40647-018-0216-0

Mandell, Laura. 2019. "Gender and Cultural Analytics: Finding or Making Stereotypes?" In *Debates in the Digital Humanities 2019*, edited by Matthew K. Gold and Lauren F. Klein. University of Minnesota Press. https://dhdebates.gc.cuny.edu/read/4805e692-0823-4073-b431-5a684250a82d/section/5d9c1b63-7b60-42dd-8cda-bde837f638f4#en30

McPherson, Tara. 2012. "Why Are the Digital Humanities So White? Or Thinking the Histories of Race and Computation." In *Debates in the Digital Humanities 2012*, edited by Matthew K. Gold. University of Minnesota Press. https://dhdebates.gc.cuny.edu/read/untitled-88c11800-9446-469b-a3be-3fdb36bfbd1e/section/b19e954b-71eb-4fca-a7a7-7dce78d24dc1#cover

Moretti, Franco. 2013. *Distant Reading*. Verso.

Noble, Safiya Umoja. 2018. *Algorithms of Oppression: How Search Engines Reinforce Racism*. New York University Press. https://nyupress.org/9781479837243/algorithms-of-oppression

Noble, Safiya Umoja. 2019. "Toward a Critical Black Digital Humanities." In *Debates in the Digital Humanities 2019*, edited by Matthew K. Gold and Lauren F. Klein. University of Minnesota Press. https://dhdebates.gc.cuny.

edu/read/untitled-f2acf72c-a469-49d8-be35-67f9ac1e3a60/section/5aafe7fe-db7e-4ec1-935f-09d8028a2687#ch02

Nyhan, Julianne, and Melissa Terras. 2017. "Uncovering 'Hidden' Contributions to the History of Digital Humanities: The Index Thomisticus' Female Keypunch Operators." In *Digital Humanities 2017*, 313–315. Montreal, QC, Canada. https://discovery.ucl.ac.uk/id/eprint/10052279/

O'Neil, Cathy. 2016. *Weapons of Math Destruction: How Big Data Increases Inequality and Threatens Democracy*. Penguin.

O'Sullivan, James. 2017. "Computing Differences in Language between Male and Female Authors." *RTÉ Brainstorm*, October 18. https://www.rte.ie/eile/brainstorm/2017/1018/913307-computing-differences-in-language-between-male-and-female-authors/

O'Sullivan, James. 2023. "DH Pedagogy in Ireland as Neo-Liberal Logic or Social Opportunity?" In *Digital Humanities 2023: Book of Abstracts*, 474. Graz, Austria. https://zenodo.org/record/7961822

Posner, Miriam. 2012. "Think Talk Make Do: Power and the Digital Humanities." *Journal of Digital Humanities* 1 (2). http://journalofdigitalhumanities.org/1-2/think-talk-make-do-power-and-the-digital-humanities-by-miriam-posner/

Prescott, Andrew. 2016. "What Price Gale Cengage?" Digital Riffs (blog). 2016. https://medium.com/digital-riffs/what-price-gale-cengage-668d358ce5cd

Ramsay, Stephen. 2013. "On Building." In *Defining Digital Humanities*, edited by Melissa Terras, Julianne Nyhan, and Edward Vanhoutte, 243–245. Ashgate.

Rhody, Lisa Marie. 2016. "Why I Dig: Feminist Approaches to Text Analysis." In *Debates in the Digital Humanities 2016*, edited by Matthew K. Gold and Lauren F. Klein. University of Minnesota Press. https://dhdebates.gc.cuny.edu/read/untitled/section/508c8664-15c8-4262-a72a-e49299873d11

Risam, Roopika. 2018a. *New Digital Worlds: Postcolonial Digital Humanities in Theory, Praxis, and Pedagogy*. Evanston, IL: Northwestern University Press.

Risam, Roopika. 2018b. "What Passes for Human?: Undermining the Universal Subject in Digital Humanities Praxis." In *Bodies of Information: Intersectional Feminism and the Digital Humanities*, edited by Elizabeth Losh and Jacqueline Wernimont, 39–56. University of Minnesota Press. doi:10.5749/j.ctv9hj9r9.6

Ross, Shawna, and Andrew Pilsch, eds. 2019. *Humans at Work in the Digital Age: Forms of Digital Textual Labor*. Routledge.

Ruberg, Bonnie, Jason Boyd, and James Howe. 2018. "Toward a Queer Digital Humanities." In *Bodies of Information: Intersectional Feminism and the Digital Humanities*, edited by Elizabeth Losh and Jacqueline Wernimont, 108–128. University of Minnesota Press. doi:10.5749/j.ctv9hj9r9.11

Rybicki, Jan. 2016. "Vive La Différence: Tracing the (Authorial) Gender Signal by Multivariate Analysis of Word Frequencies." *Digital Scholarship in the Humanities* 31 (4): 746–761. doi:10.1093/llc/fqv023

Smithies, James. 2023. "The Dark Side of DH." In *The Bloomsbury Handbook to the Digital Humanities*, edited by James O'Sullivan, 111–121. London: Bloomsbury Academic. https://kclpure.kcl.ac.uk/portal/en/publications/the-dark-side-of-dh

Unsworth, John. 2002. "What Is Humanities Computing and What Is Not?" Forum Computerphilologie. http://computerphilologie.digital-humanities.de/jg02/unsworth.html

Weidman, Sean G., and James O'Sullivan. 2018. "The Limits of Distinctive Words: Re-Evaluating Literature's Gender Marker Debate." *Digital Scholarship in the Humanities* 33 (2): 374–390. doi:10.1093/llc/fqx017

Weizenbaum, Joseph. 1977. *Computer Power and Human Reason: From Judgement to Calculation*. W. H. Freeman & Co.

Zuboff, Shoshana. 2019. *The Age of Surveillance Capitalism: The Fight for a Human Future at the New Frontier of Power.* Profile Books.

7

DIGITAL HUMANITIES FUTURES

The digital humanities have had something of a Kino-esque past, but that tradition ended with the arrival of the "DH moment" (Gold 2012). While there are still some individuals and small, low-budget cooperative initiatives at work, DH can no longer lean into the underdog narrative that long served the field well (Nyhan and Flinn 2016). The digital humanities are in the spotlight now—it is possible we are even in the "post-DH moment"—and its practitioners must decide what to do with all of the resources they have secured, all the jobs that have been created, and all of the departments and centres that have been established. This transformation from margin to mainstream presents both opportunities and dangers that will shape the field's future. Whatever might be said of the DH past, the future of DH is one which demands very careful consideration, because whether one likes it or not, the field is rapidly expanding.

DH's future depends not on perpetual innovation but on developing sustainable practices grounded in humanistic values. There are three potential futures for the field: dissolution into existing disciplines, transformation into a service function for other humanities fields, or evolution into a mature discipline with

DOI: 10.4324/9781351203395-7

its own methods and values. The most promising path forward requires DH to prioritise understanding over innovation, develop genuinely inclusive practices, and maintain critical distance from the technologies it employs. The future of DH lies not in technological determinism but in fostering critical computational literacy, the ability to both use and critique digital tools in service of humanistic inquiry.

In *The Innovation Delusion*, Lee Vinsel and Andrew L. Russell argue that the ideology of change that is now rampant in society has led to the disintegration of vital activities like "maintenance" and "care" (Vinsel and Russell 2020). In the quest to make everything new, we have forgotten to nurture that which is essential, that which, regardless of any new innovations, will still require upkeep. This insight is particularly urgent for DH, where the pursuit of the next tool or method often abandons still-functional projects and approaches. Vinsel and Russell focus on computer science, where most programs now emphasise design and programming, when, in reality, most jobs in the tech industry remain in hardware-related roles, in IT and the upkeep of systems. If the age of generative AI has taught us anything, it should be that blue-sky thinkers are of little use to anyone if everyday infrastructures, technical or otherwise, are unreliable and unsustainable. When envisioning the future of DH, and many scholars are doing just that (Prescott 2015), it would be useful to keep such lessons in mind.

The maintenance crisis in DH is already visible in the graveyard of abandoned projects, broken links, and obsolete platforms discussed throughout this book. A sustainable future requires acknowledgment of this problem and developing practices to address it.

In the conclusion to the essay from which this chapter takes its name, Amy E. Earhart cites Rosanne G. Potter, who, in 1989, called for "a new kind of literary study absolutely comfortable with scientific methods yet completely suffused with the values of the humanities" (Earhart 2016). It cannot be said that Potter's vision has been realised, and decades later, we are still faced with two cultures thinking, the digital humanities versus the (non-digital) humanities. This persistent division suggests that the problem is not merely institutional inertia but reflects deeper epistemological tensions. To use the phrase "two cultures" might be exaggerating the current divide, and certainly, there are those who believe that DH is now normative (Underwood 2019; Drucker 2023), which is a start. But we are still a long way from DH work being cited by those in the wider humanities; we are still a long way from some of the big, "traditional" humanities journals considering research based on computer-assisted methods, and we are a still a long way from everyone understanding that DH really has very little, if anything, to do with websites. And most importantly, the antagonism continues: those outside DH continue to accuse the field of suffocating existing disciplines, and those inside continue to put up barriers to so-called charlatans and lash out at naysayers. For a long time, both DH advocates and their critics have tended to frame their work in ways that align with what funders and institutions most readily reward, often at the expense of slower forms of humanistic argument and mutual intelligibility across subfields. Escaping this dynamic requires structural changes in how we evaluate and fund humanities research, so that digital and non-digital approaches are not positioned as rivals but as different modes of inquiry that can inform one another. Earhart proposes a way forward: "We need to work together, in the shared spaces, to develop working models that best articulate our hopes" (Earhart 2016). It is the idea of *shared* spaces that makes Earhart's position so compelling, because it acknowledges the difference between DH and its others. But what would these shared spaces look like in practice, and who controls their design? There will always be those who think that "digital humanities" is just a collective term for computer-assisted methodologies in the humanities. And there will always be those who think the term redundant in an age where everything is done with computers. But such views—particularly, the latter perspective—neglect a whole generation of scholars who have been trained in formally-constituted DH programs, current and coming generations who see DH as their *discipline.* This means that, for the medium-term future at least, there will always be a difference between DH and the humanities, because the DH-specific generation have come up learning different things as part of a different disciplinary culture. There will be humanities scholars who sometimes venture into DH, there will be humanities scholars who never venture into DH, and there will be DH scholars who do and do not see themselves as part of the "other" humanities. And provided these cohorts can learn to co-exist, to meet in the "shared spaces," everything should be fine. One can be optimistic about such a future, because while there is a difference between the humanities and the digital humanities, there is also a lasting epistemological exchange: we know the digital humanities because we know the humanities, and vice versa. They are one but different, and in a constant state of reciprocal flux. This reciprocal relationship, however, is not equal. As examined in previous chapters, DH often operates from a position of institutional privilege that shapes these exchanges in problematic ways.

Moreover, as a discipline, DH will need discipline-specific values (Spiro 2012). But such values should not be mired in the delusional language of innovation, and while there is room for new ideas, there can be no future for the digital humanities if that future is not committed to maintaining, upkeeping, and caring for the values of the humanities as they existed before machines. This raises a crucial question: which humanistic values should be preserved, and which need transformation? The humanities' own history includes exclusions and biases that digital methods sometimes amplify. As Underwood explains, while we are generally led to believe that the power of numbers lies in their ability to measure objective fact, this is a "folk maxim," and numbers and the algorithms that deal in them "don't inherently promise objectivity." Statistical and computer-assisted ways of reading can be valuable for those in the humanities, "not as objective oracles, but as ways of representing parallax and historical change" (Underwood 2020). If the future of DH is one which remains enamoured with "innovation" and "newness," it will probably be a poorer future built on the false promise of the quantitative. Computers, algorithms, statistics, machine learning; gen AI can produce a future that either re-energises or replaces human perspective and intuition. The former seems a far more desirable pursuit. But desirability and likelihood are two different things. Current institutional pressures push strongly toward replacement rather than augmentation.

Patrik Svensson believes that DH should serve as a space, or what he calls a "laboratory," for examining the current state and future of the humanities (Svensson 2012). Such an ethos would ensure that the digital humanities remain anchored in the foundational values of the humanities, even as the field develops its own methods and priorities. DH would thus retain its distinctiveness while remaining accountable to the intellectual traditions from which it emerged. This ethos advocates "dedicating the digital humanities to the soul of the humanities" (Liu 2013). The future of DH would thus be occupied with the question: what should we be doing in the humanities, and how can computers help? Liu's formulation is appealing but risks positioning DH as merely auxiliary to "real" humanities work. A more radical vision might ask: how do digital methods transform what counts as humanistic inquiry? This does not mean, as it might seem at first sight, that those in DH spend their time thinking about how they might "improve" or "save" the humanities. These questions assume that the humanities do not need saving, and if they do, they are more than capable of saving themselves. These questions are framed for the benefit of DH, so that its practitioners might remember that the aims and values of the humanities should act as a barometer throughout their endeavours. If scholars in the wider humanities find value in these reflections, that is welcome. But the responsibility articulated here lies with DH itself: to define its aims clearly and to remain accountable to the humanistic values it invokes.

Modelling the future in this way would retain the two cultures, but far less antagonistically. Humanities scholars could continue to do the work that has served culture and society so well for so long, while digital humanities could continue to explore how computers can contribute to the task of exploring the human condition. Both groups will be guided by the values of the humanities, and both groups will exchange perspective and critical skills as needed. This vision of peaceful coexistence may be too optimistic. Power differentials, resource competition, and epistemological conflicts suggest that tension between these cultures is structural, not accidental. As that exchange becomes more harmonious, our obsession with disciplinary boundaries will lessen. Disciplinary boundaries, provided they are fluid and can be crossed, are not necessarily a bad thing, and serve a great many cultural and administrative functions. But an obsession with them, as has sometimes been seen in DH, can be problematic, as it creates unnecessary divisions. If the future of the DH is intentionally guided by the humanities, then perhaps the humanities might ease up on the (sometimes) unnecessary resistance, and take a moment to enquire of informed colleagues and writings what sophisticated digital tools and methods might do for their research agenda. When all of this begins to happen more frequently, scholars and practitioners on both sides will come to realise for themselves what Underwood has already told us: "A method becomes humanistic not when it has the right philosophical character but when it is in fact used by humanists" (Underwood 2020, 107). But who counts as a humanist in this formulation? As previous chapters have shown, DH often excludes those without technical training or institutional resources. A truly humanistic DH must grapple with these exclusions.

For the digital humanities to secure a meaningful future, it must justify its intellectual and social value beyond academic contexts, clarifying how its methods and insights contribute to public culture, civic life, and professional practice outside the university. The value of DH lies in its capacity to cultivate critical computational literacy, the ability to understand how digital systems structure knowledge, culture, and power, and to intervene in those systems with humanistic insight. If DH is to justify itself beyond the academy, it must demonstrate that it equips students and publics to challenge and reshape digital technologies. Now that we have started teaching digital humanities to undergraduates, students who, for the most part, will not be going on to careers in academia, we need to give serious consideration to what it is we are teaching when we teach DH.[1] What can the DH graduate bring to their community, their society, their culture, their workplaces?

This question is more than an exercise in curricular design; it is about defining the social and professional utility of DH in an era where digital literacy is no longer an optional skill but a fundamental requirement. Digital literacy itself is a contested term that often obscures more than it reveals. What kind of digital literacy does DH promote, and whose interests does it serve? The DH graduate should not merely leave university with an appreciation of how computational methods intersect with humanistic inquiry; they must be equipped with the critical and technical skills necessary to navigate and shape the digital world. Whether they work in tech companies, cultural institutions, government, or community organisations, they should be able to interrogate digital infrastructures, assess the biases of algorithmic systems, and contribute to the ethical design and implementation of digital techniques.

This requires a shift in how DH is framed pedagogically. It cannot be taught as a purely academic discipline, one that orbits within scholarly debates while ignoring the applied realities of digital work beyond the university. Nor can it be reduced to a set of vocationally oriented technical skills, stripping it of the theoretical and critical dimensions that make it an intellectual enterprise. Instead, DH must be positioned as a discipline that teaches its students to be both makers and critics of digital culture, to understand not just how digital tools work, but why they matter and what power structures they reinforce. This pedagogical vision connects to larger questions about DH's social function. In an era of surveillance capitalism, algorithmic bias, and persistent digital divides, DH practitioners bear responsibilities that extend beyond methodological innovation. They have a duty to interrogate the infrastructures that shape public knowledge, to make their methods and data legible and accountable, to resist extractive research practices, and to contribute to more equitable digital cultures. This means designing projects that serve communities rather than merely studying them, foregrounding transparency in computational work, and teaching forms of digital literacy that empower rather than mystify.

If DH is to establish itself as a field with enduring relevance, it must demonstrate that its graduates are not only well-versed in computational techniques but also able to apply those techniques in ways that are socially responsible, ethically sound, and culturally engaged. It means producing graduates who can ask difficult questions about digital rights, critical AI, and the politics of the digital. It means a DH that matters, not just in the academy, but in the world at large. But what does it mean for DH to matter? This question requires examining specific examples of engaged DH work.

This question can be answered most clearly by looking at engaged DH projects such as *Torn Apart / Separados* and *Industrial Memories*, both examined shortly below, which combine methodological rigour with public responsibility. *Torn Apart / Separados* mapped the infrastructure of the United States' 2018 family-separation policy, making state violence visible as a network of institutions rather than an abstraction. *Industrial Memories* applies cultural analytics to Ireland's archival record of institutional child abuse, using computational methods to identify patterns across testimonies while retaining the specificity of individual experience. Such projects demonstrate how DH can render structures of power legible and scale interpretation without reducing lived experience to data.

Regardless of what the general public or policymakers might think, many of us know the value of the humanities, how art and literature enable individuals to reflect on themselves and their place in the world, how theory challenges assumptions by proposing new perspectives, how writing can capture what has been or compel one to feel. What can the digital, and its acolytes, bring to all of that? How can we ensure that the future DH is "a DH that matters" (Gold and Klein 2019)?

Looking back on the history of the digital humanities, the early generations had a real sense of what they were about, what made them different. As DH became institutionalised, its early identification with marginality could no longer be sustained in the same way. This does not mean that radical scholarship disappears, and indeed, other areas of the humanities demonstrate the opposite, but that the conditions under which radicalism operates are transformed. But there is now a danger that DH is becoming a little stale, and that the current generation now needs a few trailblazers to set what is happening now from that which came before. This staleness reflects not just generational change but the institutionalisation of once-radical practices. When DH becomes a degree program with learning outcomes and assessment rubrics, how can it maintain its transformative edge? Certainly, new machine-learning techniques are producing findings that would have been difficult or impossible a decade ago, but in many respects this remains a continuation of long-standing DH practices, now supported by more powerful computation. Is steady refinement of existing tools enough? That depends on what we think DH is for, and if DH aspires to reshape humanistic inquiry in the digital age, incremental improvements in text analytics alone will not suffice.

Perhaps the future of DH belongs to theory, something which was resisted in the past for fear that the knowledge that comes from craft and making would be "swallowed in postmodernisms" (Rockwell 2013, 249–250). It is possible that this turn is already underway, and the more it happens, the more DH will be positioned to answer Johanna Drucker's call and reclaim the cultural authority of digital technology from the sciences and engineering (Drucker 2012). Safiya Umoja Noble echoes Drucker: "Is the narrow, inwardly focused attention on institutionalizing digital humanities to the exclusion of the social, political, and economic landscape worth it?" (Noble 2019).

As theory continues to creep in, the emergence of distinct communities identifying as "computational humanities," "cultural analytics," and "computational literary studies" may well become the refuge for those who favour the technical forms of DH. This splintering might seem like failure, but it could also represent healthy differentiation: different approaches for different questions. Or perhaps we are finally arriving at the post-DH moment in which the critical, theoretical, and technical are spread across a range of disciplines, some of which think of themselves as DH, while others remain more closely connected to alternative lineages in corpus and computational linguistics, media studies, or the broader computational social sciences. DH does not have to be a distinct, cohesive field, it can also be used to describe a diffuse set of approaches and methodologies that different disciplines adopt when appropriate, integrating computational techniques into their own established epistemologies.

Rather than continuing to fight for disciplinary legitimacy, DH, or whatever remains of it, might gradually be absorbed into the intellectual fabric of the humanities at large, its tools and methods becoming routine elements of scholarly practice rather than treated as exceptional interventions. Such "naturalisation" would not eliminate theory, for no discipline operates without one, but would signal a shift in emphasis: theoretical debates would surface most sharply when digital methods generate friction or reveal limits, rather than as constant boundary-defining exercises. If DH dissolves into various disciplinary formations, does it risk losing the particular configuration of critique that has marked its development, that insistence on examining not only cultural artefacts but also the technical and institutional systems through which those artefacts are produced, circulated, and interpreted? One of the defining strengths of DH has been its willingness to interrogate the ideological underpinnings of digital technologies and their entanglements with capital and power. If the field splinters, does this intellectual project weaken? Or does it, conversely, allow for a more meaningful integration of digital methods across the humanities, where computation is no longer an add-on but a fundamental component of humanistic inquiry? These questions become more urgent when we consider how DH might address real-world problems. The following projects suggest what socially-engaged DH futures might look like.

Regardless of whether DH continues to be called DH, many positive DH futures—even positive post-DH futures—are possible. Roopika Risam suggests that the digital humanities might be used to realise a social justice-oriented approach to digital knowledge production:

> We can do it. We have the ability, knowledge, and tools to build new worlds. The potential for digital humanities lies in its capacity for worldmaking—for using digital humanities scholarship to create new models for knowledge and the world. These approaches must acknowledge how the cultural record has been shaped by racism and colonialism, and they must redress the ways that digital knowledge production is implicated in these forces.
>
> (Risam 2018, 142)

Risam's claim is deliberately aspirational, but it is not naïve. Her emphasis on worldmaking foregrounds the capacity of digital scholarship to reshape how knowledge is structured and legitimised. To acknowledge that the cultural record has been shaped by racism and colonialism is to recognise that datasets and platforms are never neutral.

If DH is to participate in worldmaking, it must do so by redesigning infrastructures, rethinking metadata and classification, foregrounding governance and data ownership, and centring communities historically excluded from digital knowledge production. This requires working within existing systems to expose and reconfigure them, rather than either celebrating or rejecting digital technologies wholesale. In this sense, Risam's vision is a rigorous ethical demand: that digital humanities align its technical practices with the project of historical reckoning and redress.

Risam, alongside Manan Ahmed, Maira E. Álvarez, Sylvia A. Fernández, Alex Gil, Merisa Martinez, Moacir P. de Sá Pereira, Linda Rodriguez, and other contributors, illustrate what such a future might yield in their *Torn Apart / Separados* project, a "critical data and visualization intervention" in the 2018 "Zero Tolerance Policy" adopted by the United States government towards asylum seekers.[2] The project demonstrates how DH can respond rapidly to urgent political situations, using digital methods not for their own sake but to expose and resist injustice. By mapping ICE facilities and contractors, the project makes visible the infrastructure of family separation, transforming abstract policy into concrete, locatable reality.

Another example would be the *Industrial Memories* project at University College Dublin, led by Emilie Pine, Mark Keane, and Susan Leavy, which uses cultural analytics to examine "Ireland's legacy of institutional child abuse."[3] This project shows how computational methods can give voice to trauma that might otherwise remain hidden in archives. By analysing testimonies at scale, the project identifies patterns of abuse while maintaining respect for individual experiences.

Also, *The Quipu Project* shines a light on how former president of Peru, Alberto Fujimori, "launched a new family planning programme that resulted in the sterilisation of 272,028 women and 22,004 men."[4] Using an Andean recording system as its interface metaphor, the project demonstrates how DH can decolonise its own methods, drawing on non-Western knowledge systems to tell stories of violence and resistance.

These projects share several characteristics that point toward viable DH futures: they address specific injustices rather than abstract problems; they use methods appropriate to their materials and communities; they prioritise impact over innovation; and they understand technology as always already political.

The tone adopted in writings like the oft-cited *Digital Humanities Manifesto 2.0*, with its image of DH as that which "affirms the value of the open, the infinite, the expansive, the university/museum/archive/library without walls" and "the democratization of culture and scholarship" (Schnapp et al. 2009), always seems a little overstated, if not naïve. The manifesto's language reflects a particular moment of technological optimism that now seems dated. Post-Cambridge Analytica, post-surveillance capitalism, can we still believe in the "democratising" power of the digital? While any manifesto should be aspirational, good ones tend to be achievable, and set out some sort of path to the future proposed. It is unlikely that DH will ever deliver the utopia envisioned by some of its more positive advocates, but in projects like *Torn Apart / Separados* and *Industrial Memories*, we do find concrete examples of social justice work being done in the name of DH, using robust, sustainable digital infrastructures and statistical methods, and that is at least a start. More of the same would also be a future worth pursuing. But even these exemplary projects face challenges that illuminate broader issues about DH's future.

DH has been charged with contributing to a "cloud of ignorance," detaching students and scholars from "the history and culture around them" (Golumbia 2016). If we are to escape the logic of contemporary culture and society, we need understanding, and there is very little understanding nowadays without some understanding of the digital. This presents a paradox: we need digital knowledge to critique digital culture, but acquiring that knowledge risks reinforcing the very structures we seek to challenge. How do we develop critical digital literacy without becoming complicit? Maybe this is the future DH we should seek, one of understanding, on all sides. Students and scholars need to better understand the software systems that are mediating our existence, and how their negative impacts might be suppressed, or even better, reconstituted for the purposes of new forms of reading, new forms of expression, and new forms of socially-just knowledge production. Such a future may prove difficult, and its pursuit may expose the humanities to further institutional strain, but retreating from the attempt would leave the design of digital culture entirely to others. If DH is to matter, it must engage this terrain despite the risks.

A future built on understanding of digital systems, of algorithms, of machines, of gen AI, of this discipline and its malcontents, would strengthen the digital humanities by moving it gradually away from manifesto language or institutional branding. Returning one last time to Stephen Ramsay, spirit and scholarship are not the same thing, and to speak of DH futures where "everyone is included," where "it's all about community and comity, collaboration and cooperation" (Ramsay 2013, 240), is really to speak of no future at all. Ramsay's critique of feel-good rhetoric remains sharp, but we must ask: what would genuine inclusion look like? Not everyone holding hands, but perhaps everyone having access to the tools and training needed to participate meaningfully in digital culture. These obscure ideals and sentiments do nothing to progress the field. Sentiment offers little of the "merciless introspection" that Earhart reminds us is necessary to challenge existing power structures (Earhart 2016). Sentiment does little to satisfy Julia Flanders, who asks that we seek "a model for how humanists might work at scale without losing sight of why our study matters" (Flanders 2013). Sentiment does not present and resolve the grand challenges which any meaningful DH future must identify and contend with (Prescott 2023). Sentiment, though couched in the language of inclusion, does nothing to change the position of anyone, showing those who want to do the work of DH how they might go about it, or how those already doing it might improve upon their craft.

The digital humanities have enough "community" and "collaboration." As this book has attempted to show, DH's future depends less on expanding its networks and more on clarifying its intellectual foundations: its epistemologies, ontologies, methods, tools, and theoretical commitments. This understanding must be both technical and critical: knowing how systems work and why they work that way, who benefits and who is harmed. To practise DH responsibly requires understanding the digital technologies one deploys at the level of structure and limitation. Algorithms interface with interpretation by shaping what counts as evidence; data models interface with archives by determining what can be represented; platforms interface with public humanities by mediating access and visibility. Technical literacy, then, is one of the conditions under which humanistic inquiry now operates. That seems like a very obvious thing, and maybe it is the field's present, but if not, it should certainly be its future:

> Coding can be as mindless as any other task, and knowing how to make things work does not guarantee insight. But ideological critique and critical studies of media also reach a limit without some knowledge of technological underpinning.
>
> (Burdick et al. 2012, 116)

Or, to put it a little more bluntly:

> When historians applied psychoanalysis to historical subjects, we did not suggest they "collaborate" with psychoanalysts and then test their statements against the historical record to see how much they held true; instead, historians themselves worked to deploy concepts that were seen as themselves meaningful.
>
> (Schmidt 2016)

Schmidt's analogy reveals a crucial point: true interdisciplinarity requires more than collaboration—it requires scholars to develop genuine expertise across domains. This has implications for how we train future DH practitioners. A DH future built on understanding would require clear standards to articulate what meaningful engagement entails. Interdisciplinarity does not eliminate boundaries; it makes them explicit. To work across domains responsibly requires demonstrable competence in the methods one deploys and the theories one invokes. Establishing shared expectations about technical literacy and methodological transparency would not close DH off from others, but would clarify what counts as rigorous practice within it.

Collaboration is dangerously privileged; it takes money and time and access to networks. The fetishisation of collaboration often masks how it reinforces existing hierarchies. Those with resources can afford to collaborate; those without must work alone or not at all. The digital humanities have lost and will continue to lose brilliant ideas if we continue to rely on entitled ideals like collaboration and limited black-box tools that cannot adapt to the nuances of the questions we ask in the humanities. Every time a student or scholar abandons an idea because they cannot find or afford a suitable collaborator or tool, the future of the digital humanities becomes a little more impoverished. Understanding does not resolve this issue, but alleviates it greatly.

Finally, understanding will bring acceptance: "If quantitative methods don't conflict with humanists" existing theories of interpretation, why has controversy on the topic been so fierce? I believe the real problem is that new methods remain inaccessible" (Underwood 2020, 107). But accessibility is not just about technical knowledge. It is about whose questions get asked, whose methods get validated, whose work gets recognised. The following section examines what threatens these more inclusive futures.

There is much threatening the future of the digital humanities. The discipline is often its own worst enemy, incapable of accepting criticism or facing up to difficult questions. Where there was once a "DH community" of a sort there are now firm epistemological camps, which is natural and expected in such an expansive field, but these differing schools expend far too much energy weighing themselves against and seeking to undermine their counterparts: the theorists think the coders are just technicians, and the coders think the theorists are just failed critics. These divisions reflect deeper anxieties about what constitutes legitimate knowledge in the digital age. When everyone claims to do "real"

DH, no one does. In her response to Nan Z. Da's critique of computational literary studies (Da 2019), Katherine Bode asks: "What would it take to bridge the scholarly and critical—the curatorial and statistical—dimensions of (digital) literary studies and what alternative, shared futures for our discipline could result?" (Bode 2019). The same question could be asked of many of the DH sub-fields.

Geoffrey Rockwell writes of "disciplinary violence," using the story of Romulus and Remus as a cautionary tale of how "founders never think of their foundational work as a violence" (Rockwell 2013, 250). But who decides where the walls should be, and who remains outside them? The violence of boundary-drawing in DH continues, often enacted by those who claim to oppose it. When Romulus killed Remus (returning to Rome), he was defending the walls of his new city, much like the digital humanities once had to defend itself from disciplinary perspectives that did not understand its nature and community, its configuration as a site for academics and para-academics alike, for "programmers, librarians, computing support staff, graphic designers and so on" (Rockwell 2013, 250). As we continue to have the "what is DH?" discussion, as DH continues to become even more concrete, more an accepted part of higher education, the more likely it is that we "delegitimize the non-textual forms of making knowledge important to those who implement and maintain information systems" (Rockwell 2013, 251). Rockwell, as something of a DH founder himself, is fearful of those who "value theoretical discourse over practice" (Rockwell 2013, 251), but he, unlike Romulus, has the self-awareness to see that exclusion—disciplinary violence—is not the way to respond to such fear. The ideal future for the digital humanities, he posits, is one in which "the theoretical and the pragmatic can inform each other without participants needing to excel at both" (Rockwell 2013, 251). And in the succeeding years, that situation has partly been realised. The tension between theory and practice continues to structure debates about DH's future. Perhaps the problem is the binary itself, as if theory and practice were separable rather than mutually constituting.

It is very hard to predict what is coming next, and that is part of what makes DH such an exciting field. The emergence of gen

AI and intriguing new language models that use deep learning, or powerful, increasingly affordable devices for augmented and virtual reality, promise so much. But we have heard such promises before. Each new technology is heralded as transformative, yet the fundamental questions remain unchanged. Such promise often comes to nothing, but for all those gadgets and techniques that pass quietly to the museum of dead technologies, there are a small few that radically shift the ways in which we see and think about our cultures and humanity. And the future of DH is not dependent on some "new big thing," some "grand innovation"; there are existing datasets, methods, tools, techniques, and theories that need to be validated, improved, and refined. And there is an endless supply of cultural materials to which our existing tools and techniques are ready to be applied. If technology stopped progressing at this very moment, those working in the digital humanities would have enough to keep them going for a very long time to come. This stability, however, should not breed complacency. The work to be done includes not just applying existing methods but interrogating their limitations and biases.

Alan Liu's "Map of DH"[5] visualises how the digital humanities operates at the intersection between fields like literary studies, history, media studies, media arts, and design. Liu represents the interdisciplinarity through an ontological network, where media studies is located near media archaeology which is connected to the history of the book which is part of both literary studies and history. Many of these domains share common methodologies and theories, such as distant reading, modelling theory, and design.

People are growing tired of the conversations provoked by undertakings like the "Map of DH," but this is important work and we need to keep defining and to keep mapping. The exhaustion with definitional debates reflects a desire to move beyond meta-discourse to "real work." But the meta-discourse is real work: it shapes what questions can be asked and whose work counts. Rather than moving beyond these conversations, we need to turn back into them, because if DH continues to expand unhindered, it will probably collapse in on itself. Encouraging further conversation allows for evaluation; it allows for the introduction of news, the reconsideration of old perspectives. Stopping the "what is DH?" conversation now suggests that there is something comfortable in the status quo, leaving the discipline to stagnate as it moves towards whatever future awaits.

The urgency of continued definition becomes clear when we consider how emerging technologies are reshaping the field. Generative AI, large language models, immersive media, and increasingly automated research workflows alter what counts as authorship, evidence, interpretation, and even reading itself. As these technologies reorganise scholarly labour and mediate first encounters with texts and archives, they blur distinctions between analysis and generation, assistance and substitution. Without sustained definitional work, DH risks either absorbing every new technological development uncritically or reacting defensively to it. While many may seek to frame it as self-indulgent meta-discourse, ongoing clarification of DH's epistemic commitments is a necessary condition for responsible adaptation.

It is likely that generative AI will be a major part of that future, but Underwood does not think that future will represent a radical break from the present, and that large language models are succeeding the internet as the primary tool through which we organise knowledge (Underwood 2024). This shift is already visible in how students approach research: ChatGPT before Google, synthesis before search. What happens to humanistic inquiry when AI mediates our first encounter with texts and ideas? Like all disciplines, DH must adapt to account for the epistemological shifts that generative AI introduces. If large language models are indeed becoming the dominant means of organising knowledge, then the role of DH in interrogating these systems: examining their biases, their limitations, and their effects on cultural production becomes more critical than ever. Rather than retreating from definitional debates, we should be using them as a lens to explore how AI is reshaping the boundaries of humanistic inquiry.

DH has always been concerned with mediation, with how digital tools influence interpretation and meaning-making. Generative AI represents another phase in this ongoing transformation, producing a new set of challenges that demand critical engagement. If we prematurely abandon the question of what DH is, we risk allowing AI to dictate its evolution without the necessary scrutiny. Instead of disengaging, we must turn our attention to how DH can contribute to a deeper understanding of AI's role in structuring knowledge, ensuring that the discipline remains not only relevant but essential in shaping the future of humanistic scholarship.

The digital humanities can leverage generative AI both as an analytical tool and as a means of producing new forms of scholarly output. Large language models can assist in text analysis by identifying patterns, summarising large corpora, and generating hypotheses that scholars can refine through close reading. AI can augment traditional distant reading methods, providing a way to compare thematic, stylistic, or rhetorical trends across vast datasets more efficiently. Additionally, generative AI can facilitate multimodal analysis, enabling the synthesis of textual, visual, and audio data in ways that were previously cumbersome or resource intensive. But each of these applications raises questions about interpretation and the displacement of human judgement. When an AI identifies a pattern, who is the critic, the human who prompts it or the system that produces the output? Such capabilities can enhance the depth and scope of DH research by accelerating exploratory processes and uncovering connections that might otherwise go unnoticed.

Generative AI offers new possibilities for how DH projects communicate and present knowledge. Interactive AI-driven tools can enable dynamic engagement with archival materials, producing adaptive narratives that respond to user input. AI-generated simulations or reconstructions can offer new ways of experiencing historical and literary texts, providing immersive and speculative approaches to digital storytelling. Generative models can aid in automating aspects of annotation (Whittle et al. 2023), citation management, and draft generation, allowing scholars to focus on conceptual development rather than mechanical tasks. Automation always involves choices about what to prioritise and what to discard. The efficiency gains may come at the cost of the careful, slow attention that humanistic inquiry demands. However, as DH integrates AI into its workflows, it must also remain critically attuned to the ethical implications of these technologies, particularly in terms of authorship, bias, and the potential erosion of humanistic inquiry in favour of machine-driven efficiencies. DH's role is not just to use AI but to shape its use in ways that reflect the discipline's broader commitments to cultural critique, accessibility, and intellectual rigour.

Andrew Prescott, one of the great scholars and practitioners of the digital humanities, calls for the discipline to identify its "grand challenges" (Prescott 2023), those fundamental, large-scale problems that can define the discipline's future directions and require sustained, interdisciplinary effort to address.

DH must grapple with the management and interpretation of increasingly vast cultural datasets, ensuring that computational methodologies do not overshadow humanistic nuance. This challenge is technical but also epistemological: how do we preserve the particular in the age of the aggregate? The rise of gen AI presents both opportunities and existential questions, as machine learning and large language models increasingly determine knowledge production. DH must confront the biases embedded in digital archives and algorithms, working to decolonise data and amplify marginalised voices. But decolonisation cannot be achieved through technical fixes alone and requires fundamental restructuring of power relations within the field. Preservation and sustainability remain urgent concerns, as digital artefacts are inherently fragile and subject to corporate control and obsolescence. DH must contend, immediately, with its contribution to the climate crisis. The carbon footprint of DH—from energy-intensive computations to conference travel—contradicts its progressive values. Can we imagine a sustainable DH that does not just minimise harm but actively contributes to environmental justice?

DH struggles with institutional precarity, with many scholars navigating unstable career paths and disciplinary tensions. This precarity is not evenly distributed, falling heaviest on those already marginalised by race, gender, class, and geography. DH must fulfil its promise of public engagement, ensuring that its projects serve broader communities rather than remaining confined to academic spaces. But public engagement often becomes another form of extraction, taking community knowledge without reciprocal benefit. The ethics of digital research in the context of surveillance and privacy bring further complications, particularly as scholars work with big data and AI-driven systems that pose risks to individual rights. Traditional publishing and peer review models have yet to fully accommodate digital scholarship, limiting its visibility and impact. The slow pace of change in scholarly communication reflects deeper conservatism in how we validate knowledge.

These are the challenges which will determine whether DH remains a transformative force in the digital age or fades into obsolescence. It is in these challenges that DH will find its future. But perhaps the greatest challenge is not on Prescott's list: how to maintain hope without falling into naïve optimism, how to work for change while acknowledging the magnitude of the forces arrayed against us.

This book ends where it began, not in some nondescript piazza in Rome, but with T. S. Eliot, and his simple but powerful idea that culture, if it is to flourish, requires tension, and friction between its parts (Eliot 1949, 58). The future of the digital humanities must include the conversations and analyses that give rise to such tensions, so that we can nurture the nexus, decide and disagree and decide again what it means to use computers in the humanities with *intention*, and intention coupled with critical awareness of how our tools shape our questions, how our methods embed values, how our practices include and exclude.

The most promising futures for the digital humanities are those that embrace critical computational literacy, the ability to both use and critique digital tools, to understand their operations and their ideologies, to deploy them strategically while maintaining humanistic values. This future requires us to move beyond both naïve technophilia and reactionary technophobia toward a more nuanced understanding of how digital methods can serve humanistic inquiry without determining its direction.

Such a future demands that we take seriously the challenges identified throughout this book: the persistence of exclusion and hierarchy, the complicity with neoliberal structures, the environmental costs of our practices, the precarity of our labour. It requires us to maintain the productive tensions Eliot identified while working toward more just and sustainable practices.

Most crucially, this future requires us to remember that the "digital" in digital humanities is not an end but a means, a set of tools and methods that should enable us to ask better questions about culture and meaning in our contemporary moment. The measure of DH success will be in whether it has contributed to human understanding and flourishing. That is a future worth working towards.

RECOMMENDED READING

Allington, Daniel. 2023. "The Place of Computation in the Study of Culture." In *The Bloomsbury Handbook to the Digital Humanities*, edited by James O'Sullivan, 373–384. London: Bloomsbury Academic.

Alvarado, Rafael. 2023. "Datawork and the Future of DH." In *The Bloomsbury Handbook to the Digital Humanities*, edited by James O'Sullivan, 362–372. London: Bloomsbury Academic.

Arbuckle, Alyssa, and Ray Siemens. 2023. "Digital Humanities, Open Social Scholarship, and Engaged Publics." In *The Bloomsbury Handbook to the Digital Humanities*, edited by James O'Sullivan, 397–407. London: Bloomsbury Academic.

Berry, David M. 2011. "The Computational Turn: Thinking About the Digital Humanities." *Culture Machine* 12. https://culturemachine.net/wp-content/uploads/2019/01/10-Computational-Turn-440-893-1-PB.pdf

Earhart, Amy. 2016. "Digital Humanities Futures: Conflict, Power, and Public Knowledge." *Digital Studies/Le champ numérique* 6 (1). https://doi.org/10.16995/dscn.1

Prescott, Andrew. 2023. "The Grand Challenges of Digital Humanities." In *The Bloomsbury Handbook to the Digital Humanities*, edited by James O'Sullivan, 385–396. London: Bloomsbury Academic.

NOTES

1 This book does not deal specifically with the issue of DH pedagogy, but readers interested in this topic are very well served (Hirsch 2012; Battershill and Ross 2017; Travis and DeSpain 2018; Croxall and Jakacki 2023a; 2023b).

2 As noted in Chapter 2, see xpmethod.plaintext.in/torn-apart/volume/1/index (Volume I) and xpmethod.plaintext.in/torn-apart/volume/2/index (Volume II), or the following account of the project as published in *WIRED* magazine: Emily Dreyfuss, 'ICE Is Everywhere': Using Library Science to Map the Separation Crisis," *WIRED*, 2018, www.wired.com/story/ice-is-everywhere-using-library-science-to-map-child-separation/

3 See industrialmemories.ucd.ie

4 See interactive.quipu-project.com

5 See alanyliu.org/map-of-dh/ or prezi.com/hjkj8ztj-clv/map-of-digital-humanities/

REFERENCES

Battershill, Claire, and Shawna Ross. 2017. *Using Digital Humanities in the Classroom: A Practical Introduction for Teachers, Lecturers, and Students.* Bloomsbury Publishing.

Bode, Katherine. 2019. "Computational Literary Studies: Participant Forum Responses, Day 2." In the Moment (blog). 2019. https://critinq.wordpress.com/2019/04/02/computational-literary-studies-participant-forum-responses-day-2-3/

Burdick, Anne, Johanna Drucker, Peter Lunenfeld, Todd Presner, and Jeffrey Schnapp. 2012. *Digital_Humanities.* Cambridge: The MIT Press.

Croxall, Brian, and Diane Jakacki. 2023a. "The Invisible Labor of DH Pedagogy." In *The Bloomsbury Handbook to the Digital Humanities*, edited by James O'Sullivan, 295–304. London: Bloomsbury Academic. doi:10.17613/zfjy-w519

Croxall, Brian, and Diane K. Jakacki. 2023b. *What We Teach When We Teach DH: Digital Humanities in the Classroom.* University of Minnesota Press.

Da, Nan Z. 2019. "The Computational Case against Computational Literary Studies." *Critical Inquiry* 45 (3): 601–639. doi:10.1086/702594

Drucker, Johanna. 2012. "Humanistic Theory and Digital Scholarship." In *Debates in the Digital Humanities*, edited by Matthew K. Gold. University of Minnesota Press. https://dhdebates.gc.cuny.edu/read/untitled-88c11800-9446-469b-a3be-3fdb36bfbd1e/section/0b495250-97af-4046-91ff-98b6ea9f83c0

Drucker, Johanna. 2023. "Normative Digital Humanities." In *The Bloomsbury Handbook to the Digital Humanities*, edited by James O'Sullivan, 7–17. London: Bloomsbury Academic.

Earhart, Amy. 2016. "Digital Humanities Futures: Conflict, Power, and Public Knowledge." *Digital Studies/Le champ numérique* 6 (1). doi:10.16995/dscn.1

Eliot, T. S. 1949. *Notes Towards the Definition of Culture.* Harcourt, Brace.

Flanders, Julia. 2013. "The Literary, the Humanistic, the Digital: Toward a Research Agenda for Digital Literary Studies." In *Literary Studies in the Digital Age*, edited by Kenneth M. Price and Ray Siemens. Modern Language Association of America. https://dlsanthology.mla.hcommons.org/the-literary-the-humanistic-the-digital/

Gold, Matthew K. 2012. "The Digital Humanities Moment." In *Debates in the Digital Humanities*, edited by Matthew K. Gold. University of Minnesota Press. https://dhdebates.gc.cuny.edu/read/untitled-88c11800-9446-469b-a3be-3fdb36bfbd1e/section/fcd2121c-0507-441b-8a01-dc35b8baeec6

Gold, Matthew K., and Lauren F. Klein. 2019. "A DH That Matters." In *Debates in the Digital Humanities 2019*, edited by Matthew K. Gold and Lauren F. Klein. University of Minnesota Press. https://dhdebates.gc.cuny.edu/projects/debates-in-the-digital-humanities

Golumbia, David. 2016. "The Digital in the Humanities: An Interview with David Golumbia." Interview by Melissa Dinsman. *Los Angeles Review of Books.* https://lareviewofbooks.org/article/digital-humanities-interview-david-golumbia/

Hirsch, Brett D., ed. 2012. *Digital Humanities Pedagogy: Practices, Principles and Politics.* Open Book Publishers. doi:10.11647/OBP.0024

Liu, Alan. 2013. "The Meaning of the Digital Humanities." *PMLA* 128 (2): 409–423. doi:10.1632/pmla.2013.128.2.409

Noble, Safiya Umoja. 2019. "Toward a Critical Black Digital Humanities." In *Debates in the Digital Humanities 2019*, edited by Matthew K. Gold and Lauren F. Klein. University of Minnesota Press. https://dhdebates.gc.cuny.edu/read/untitled-f2acf72c-a469-49d8-be35-67f9ac1e3a60/section/5aafe7fe-db7e-4ec1-935f-09d8028a2687#ch02

Nyhan, Julianne, and Andrew Flinn. 2016. "Revolutionaries and Underdogs." In *Computation and the Humanities: Towards an Oral History of Digital Humanities*, edited by Julianne Nyhan and Andrew Flinn, 257–275. Springer International Publishing. doi:10.1007/978-3-319-20170-2_17

Prescott, Andrew. 2015. "The Future and the Digital Humanities." Digital Riffs (blog). 2015. https://medium.com/digital-riffs/the-future-and-the-digital-humanities-6c6b3f8a3295

Prescott, Andrew. 2023. "The Grand Challenges of Digital Humanities." In *The Bloomsbury Handbook to the Digital Humanities*, edited by James O'Sullivan, 385–396. London: Bloomsbury Academic.

Ramsay, Stephen. 2013. "Who's In and Who's Out." In *Defining Digital Humanities*, edited by Melissa Terras, Julianne Nyhan, and Edward Vanhoutte, 239–241. Ashgate.

Risam, Roopika. 2018. *New Digital Worlds: Postcolonial Digital Humanities in Theory, Praxis, and Pedagogy*. Evanston, IL: Northwestern University Press.

Rockwell, Geoffrey. 2013. "Inclusion in the Digital Humanities." In *Defining Digital Humanities*, edited by Melissa Terras, Julianne Nyhan, and Edward Vanhoutte, 247–253. Ashgate.

Schmidt, Benjamin M. 2016. "Do Digital Humanists Need to Understand Algorithms?" In *Debates in the Digital Humanities 2016*, edited by Matthew K. Gold and Lauren F. Klein. University of Minnesota Press. https://dhdebates.gc.cuny.edu/read/untitled/section/557c453b-4abb-48ce-8c38-a77e24d3f0bd#ch48

Schnapp, Jeffrey, Todd Presner, and Peter Lunenfeld. 2009. "*Digital Humanities Manifesto* 2.0." http://jeffreyschnapp.com/wp-content/uploads/2011/10/Manifesto_V2.pdf

Spiro, Lisa. 2012. "'This Is Why We Fight': Defining the Values of the Digital Humanities." In *Debates in the Digital Humanities*, edited by Matthew K. Gold. Minneapolis: University of Minnesota Press. https://dhdebates.gc.cuny.edu/read/untitled-88c11800-9446-469b-a3be-3fdb36bfbd1e/section/9e014167-c688-43ab-8b12-0f6746095335

Svensson, Patrik. 2012. "Envisioning the Digital Humanities." *Digital Humanities Quarterly* 6 (1). http://jeffreyschnapp.com/wp-content/uploads/2011/10/Manifesto_V2.pdf

Travis, Jennifer, and Jessica DeSpain, eds. 2018. *Teaching with Digital Humanities: Tools and Methods for Nineteenth-Century American Literature*. Urbana: University of Illinois Press.

Underwood, Ted. 2019. "Digital Humanities as a Semi-Normal Thing." In *Debates in the Digital Humanities*, edited by Matthew K. Gold and Lauren F. Klein, 96–98. University of Minnesota Press. doi:10.5749/j.ctvg251hk.13

Underwood, Ted. 2020. “Machine Learning and Human Perspective.” *PMLA* 135 (1): 92–109. doi:10.1632/pmla.2020.135.1.92

Underwood, Ted. 2024. “Will AI Make Us Overconfident?” *The Stone and the Shell* (blog). August 31, 2024. https://tedunderwood.com/2024/08/31/will-ai-make-us-overconfident/

Vinsel, Lee, and Andrew L. Russell. 2020. *The Innovation Delusion: How Our Obsession with the New Has Disrupted the Work That Matters Most*. New York: Currency.

Whittle, Sophie, James O’Sullivan, and Michael Pidd. 2023. “AI and the Editor.” *The Future of Text* 4: 106–109.

Index

For Product Safety Concerns and Information please contact our EU
representative GPSR@taylorandfrancis.com
Taylor & Francis Verlag GmbH, Kaufingerstraße 24, 80331 München, Germany

www.ingramcontent.com/pod-product-compliance
Lightning Source LLC
LaVergne TN
LVHW011452121026
849885LV00033B/349
9780815384809